The Busy Attorney's Guide to
Financial Statements

Decode the Numbers, Spot Red Flags, and Protect Your Clients

RAMÓN ANDRADE

Attorney · MBA

Copyright © 2025 Ramón Andrade
All rights reserved.
ISBN: 979-8-9931910-1-0
Published by Attorney Acceleration Institute Press

Praise for The Busy Attorney's Guide to Financial Statements

"I had the privilege of working with Ramón through complex and challenging situations. His ability to integrate financial analysis with legal judgment was key. This book makes that knowledge accessible to all attorneys."

—Luis Carranza, Former CEO of CAF - Development Bank of Latin America; Former Minister of Economy and Finance, Peru

"Ramón was a key advisor to us during some of the most complex, financially sensitive matters we faced. His ability to navigate both legal and financial dimensions was instrumental—this book brings that same clarity to a broader audience of lawyers."

—Rocknee Timm, Former CEO, Gold Reserve

"As an investor, I know firsthand that financial literacy is a competitive edge. The Busy Attorney's Guide to Financial Statements bridges the gap between legal expertise and financial acumen with clarity and practicality. It equips attorneys with the tools to read beyond the numbers, uncover business realities, and confidently engage with clients, investors, and boards. For any lawyer navigating today's deal-driven world, this guide is not just useful—it's indispensable."

—Leesa Soulodre, Managing Partner, R3i Capital | Founder, Planet43 — Catalytic capital for climate, water & health (AI × deeptech), Non-Executive Director

DEDICATION

For the Virgin Mary, my mother in heaven, on her birthday.

For Carolina, my love and partner in life.

For Lourdes, my mother, and children: María Carolina, Ana Elisa, and José Ignacio.

CONTENTS

Table of Contents

PRAISE FOR THE BUSY ATTORNEY'S GUIDE TO FINANCIAL STATEMENTS iii

DEDICATION iv

CONTENTS vi

1 Introduction — Beyond the Law: Why Accounting Is Your Secret Weapon 1

2 The Accounting Principles, Assumptions, and Constraints 4

   1   Accounting Principles 5

   2   Accounting Assumptions 10

   3   Constraints 12

   4   Why These Matter for Attorneys 14

3 The Balance Sheet — Your Financial Snapshot 17

   1   The Balance Sheet Equation 20

   2   Assets — The Economic Resources 28

   3   Liabilities — The Obligations 35

   4   Equity — The Residual Claim (Net Worth) 39

   5   Financial Ratios from the Balance Sheet 43

   6   Beyond the Face: Notes, Audits, and Management Discussion & Analysis (MD&A) 47

   7   Balance Sheet Red-Flag Checklist for Lawyers 50

   8   Connecting to the Other Statements 61

   9   Stories from the Trenches 62

4 The Income Statement — Turning a Year-Long Story into One Page of Numbers 66

1	What the Income Statement Shows	69
2	Presentation Formats — Single-Step vs. Multi-Step	71
3	The Four Critical Subtotals	73
4	Line-by-Line Walk-Through and Red Flags	76
5	Income Statement Diagnostic Drill	85
6	Income Statement Margins & Coverage Ratios	86
7	Quarter-End Profit and Loss Statement ("P&L") for ABC Law LLP	92
8	Income Statement Red-Flag Checklist for Lawyers	98
9	Stories from the Trenches: When Income Statements Lie	105
10	Cash Flow Connection	106

5 The Cash-flow statement — Following the Money When Profit Isn't Cash 114

1	The Cash-flow Statement	116
2	The Three Cash Buckets	125
3	Direct vs Indirect Presentation	128
4	The Indirect Method - Step by Step	132
4.1	Start with Net Income (bottom line of the P&L)	133
4.2	Add back non-cash expenses	133
4.3	Subtract non-cash gains (e.g., unrealized FX gains).	134
4.4	Adjust for working-capital changes	134
4.5	Result: Cash Provided by Operating Activities (OCF)	136
4.6	Add the Investing and Financing sections to calculate the Net Change in Cash.	136
5	Key Cash Metrics for Lawyers	139
6	Case Illustration - ABC Law PLL, Second Quarter	143
7	Cash-flow Statement Red-Flag Checklist for Lawyers	153
8	Stories from the Trenches	158
9	How the Three Statements Talk to One Another	159
9.1	Income - Cash Flow:	159
9.2	Cash Flow -Balance Sheet:	159

9.3	Triangulation Rule:	159

6 Conclusions: From Lingering Doubt to Financial Insight – Your New Indispensable Skill 163

7 Appendices 168

Appendix A – References & Recommended Reading 168

Primary Accounting Standards & Frameworks 168
Legal & Professional References 168
Public Companies, Firms & Cases Mentioned 169
Articles & Commentary 169
Textbooks & Guides 170
Fraud & Forensic Accounting 171
Regulatory and Professional Organizations & Resources 171
Suggested Continuing Education for Attorneys 171

Appendix B – Glossary of Key Financial Terms 172

ABOUT THE AUTHOR 177

1 INTRODUCTION — BEYOND THE LAW: WHY ACCOUNTING IS YOUR SECRET WEAPON

The deal room was silent. At 11:42 p.m., with signatures due at 9 a.m., an email dropped: "minor update" to the target's balance sheet. One glance, and my pulse spiked as current liabilities had tripled. No footnote. No warning.

That single page could have sunk a deal, triggered malpractice claims, and cost our client millions. Five focused minutes with those numbers uncovered the truth and saved the transaction.

I built this book for those moments. Lawyers excel at statutes, precedent, and persuasion, yet many stumble when faced with balance sheets, income statements, or cash flow reports. While numbers can feel foreign to many lawyers, in modern practice, financial literacy is not optional; it is about survival.

What you'll learn:

- **Decode the balance sheet**: See what a business owns, owes, and the equity that remains.

- **Follow the income statement**: Track performance over time and detect manipulation.

- **Trace the cash flow**: Test whether profits translate into cash—because cash pays the bills.

- **Spot red flags**: Recognize the warning signs that precede disputes and fraud.

- **Apply ratios that matter**: Use liquidity, leverage, and cash flow metrics with confidence.

This book is not an accounting textbook. It's a lawyer's field guide: A toolkit to help you argue with numbers as well as statutes and precedent, safeguard your clients, and strengthen your career.

As you go through the book, you'll notice specific ideas appear more than once. That is intentional, so you don't need to read this book straight through. I designed it as a resource you can turn to whenever the numbers feel daunting. Repetition makes the essentials stick, and I hope that when the stakes are high, you'll have the clarity and confidence to catch the red flags and seize the opportunities hidden in the financials.

FREE BONUS: The Litigation & Due Diligence Quick Kit

As a special thank you for buying this book, I want to give you free and instant access to my 3-Point Financial Forensics Protocol.

This powerful, print-ready PDF kit includes a 5-minute diagnostic checklist, a master guide to the most dangerous red flags, and a precision reference for drafting airtight financial covenants. It's the perfect companion to keep on your desk as you go through the following chapters.

Get your free Quick Kit now at:
www.landing.ramonandrade.com/quick-kit

2 THE ACCOUNTING PRINCIPLES, ASSUMPTIONS, AND CONSTRAINTS

Chapter Thesis

Financial reporting rests on a foundation that makes business information reliable, comparable, and legally defensible. This chapter introduces the principles, assumptions, and constraints of accounting: The hidden framework behind every balance sheet, income statement, and cash flow report.

For lawyers, mastering these fundamentals means spotting manipulation, assessing risks, and strengthening arguments in disputes and negotiations.

 Chapter Snapshot – Accounting Principles, Assumptions and Constraints

Chapter Essentials

- **Principles:** Rules that guide recognition, measurement, and presentation of financial data.

- **Assumptions:** Ground rules that make financial reporting possible (e.g., going concern, periodicity).

- **Constraints:** Practical limits balancing accuracy and feasibility (e.g., cost–benefit).

- **Legal Value:** Violations generally lie at the center of disputes, litigation, and negotiations. Lawyers must recognize when principles or assumptions break down.

1 Accounting Principles

The purpose of financial reporting is to provide information about a business that is useful to investors, lenders, and other stakeholders in making economic decisions. This information is particularly important for companies with publicly traded shares, as inaccurate reporting can create market-wide consequences for investors, employees, and the broader economy.

For these purposes, accountants have developed principles and rules designed to make financial information accurate, transparent, and comparable across businesses. These principles have evolved, often refined in response to new circumstances, and unfortunately, in reaction to major corporate scandals. Names such as Enron, WorldCom, Tyco, and Lehman Brothers remind us how manipulative and fraudulent behavior has shaped reforms after causing enormous damage.

When these rules and principles gain broad acceptance, they become **generally accepted accounting principles**. Countries typically establish or recognize standard-setting bodies to codify these principles and make them available to the public. In practice, much of the world follows the **Generally Accepted Accounting Principles (GAAP)** issued by the **Financial Accounting Standards Board (FASB)** in the United States, or the **International Financial Reporting Standards (IFRS)** issued by the International **Accounting Standards Board (IASB)** based in London, the United Kingdom. These two systems dominate because they govern companies in the largest capital markets and attract the most global investors.

These generally accepted principles and standards set the framework for preparing and disclosing financial information, ensuring that financial statements remain consistent, comparable, and reliable.

1.1 Revenue Recognition (Accrual Principle)

Revenue is recorded when earned (when goods or services are provided), not when cash is received.

Example: A law firm completes $50,000 of legal work in December but invoices in January and is paid in that same month. Revenue is recognized in December.

1.2 Matching Principle
The matching principle requires expenses to be recorded in the same period as the revenue they produce.

Example: Associate salaries are matched to the revenue from the matters they work on.

1.3 Historical Cost Principle
Traditionally, assets and liabilities are recorded at historical purchase price, but modern standards increasingly allow or require fair value (market-based) measurements.

Practical Point: Attorneys should always ask which basis is being used.

1.4 Full Disclosure Principle
All information that could affect users' decisions must be disclosed in financial statements or notes.

Legal Angle: Hidden contingencies, pending lawsuits, or off–balance-sheet liabilities can dramatically alter valuations in M&A or litigation.

1.5 Consistency Principle
The same accounting methods should be used consistently from period to period unless a justified change is disclosed.

Practical Point: Look out for sudden changes in depreciation methods or inventory valuation, as they could be a sign of earnings management.

1.6 Reliability and Faithful Representation
Financial information must be free of bias or error and accurately

reflect economic reality.

Legal Angle: Attorneys should keep an incredulous attitude and look for signs that reported figures do not reflect underlying transactions (e.g., revenue "stuffing" near year-end).

1.7 Comparability

Statements must allow users to compare across time and between companies.

Example: A law firm benchmarking its profitability against industry peers relies on comparable treatment of revenue and expense recognition.

Accrual & Matching

Principle	The Rule	Why Lawyers Care	Red Flag Example
Accrual	Record revenue when earned, not when cash arrives	Premature recognition inflates damages, earn-outs, executive bonuses	December invoices for January services
Matching	Record costs in same period as related revenue	Capitalizing normal expenses props up operating profit; potential fiduciary breach	Marketing costs spread over 5 years

Table 1.1: Accrual and Matching Principles

Example — ABC Law LLP

ABC Law LLP is a small litigation boutique.

October 31: A partner completes a $20,000 brief. Even though the client won't pay until December, October's income statement records the full $20,000 revenue plus the associate's salary for the work performed. Cash timing is irrelevant; economic activity drives the recording.

The principles mentioned in this chapter 1 guide accountants in recognizing and presenting financial information, but they operate within a framework of underlying assumptions: The basic conditions that make financial reporting possible. We will review assumptions next.

2 Accounting Assumptions

While accounting principles establish the rules for recognizing, measuring, and reporting transactions, these rules are based on a deeper layer of **assumptions**.

Assumptions are the basic conditions accountants take for granted when preparing financial statements, as the ground rules that make financial reporting possible in the first place. They define the playing field: That a business is separate from its owners, that it will continue to operate in the foreseeable future, that results can be measured in a stable currency, and that time can be divided into reporting periods.

For lawyers, these assumptions are crucial because if one of them is no longer valid, for example, if a company is no longer a going concern, the entire financial statement picture changes, with significant implications for litigation, bankruptcy, and corporate governance. Understanding them also provides a framework for probing beyond surface figures, uncovering potential biases, omissions, or manipulations.

2.1 Economic Entity:

Business transactions are kept separate from those of owners or other entities.

Example: Client funds in trust should be reported on a separate balance sheet, not in your firm's balance sheet.

2.2 Going Concern:

Financial statements presume the entity will continue operating indefinitely.

Legal Angle: If liquidation looms, and thus the Going Concern assumption does not apply, asset values must drop to fire-sale prices (not historical cost) in the balance sheet, vital in bankruptcy litigation.

2.3 Materiality:

Only information that could influence decisions is reported. Both quantitative and qualitative factors matter.

Example: A $5,000 irregular payment may be quantitatively small yet qualitatively material if it is a bribe.

2.4 Conservatism (Prudence):

When in doubt, expected losses are recognized immediately, but expected gains are deferred.

Legal Angle: This assumption protects creditors and, by extension, clients in insolvency or damages disputes.

2.5 Monetary Unit:

Only transactions that can be measured in a stable currency are recorded.

Example: This becomes critical when clients hold cryptocurrencies or operate in hyperinflationary economies.

2.6 Periodicity:

The life of the business is sliced into regular reporting periods (months, quarters, years).

Legal Angle: Litigation often depends on which side of the cutoff date a transaction takes place.

While assumptions form the basis of financial reporting, they are not used in isolation. Accountants also consider practical constraints: limits that influence how these assumptions and principles are applied in the real world. Constraints, like cost–benefit considerations and industry standards, ensure that financial statements remain both useful and realistic.

3 Constraints

In practice, accountants operate within a set of **constraints** that balance theoretical accuracy with real-world practicality.

Some textbooks treat **materiality** and **conservatism** as constraints; in this book, we have included them under assumptions because they shape how accountants approach recognition and measurement. The constraints discussed here instead focus on the practical boundaries that guide reporting in context, such as cost–benefit considerations and industry practices.

For lawyers, these constraints matter because disputes typically arise not from outright violations of principles, but from disagreements over how far these practical limits should be stretched, such as whether disclosure costs outweigh their benefits or whether an industry-specific practice justifies a deviation from general rules.

3.1 Cost–Benefit (or Cost Constraint)

The value of information disclosed should exceed the cost of providing it.

Legal Angle: Useful in litigation or disclosure disputes, where one side argues that omission of information was justified by excessive cost.

3.2 Industry Practice

Sometimes, general accounting principles are adjusted to the needs of a particular industry. In these cases, the industry-adapted reporting provides more relevant information.

Example: Accepted accounting practices adapt general rules to reflect the particulars of law firms and their business. For instance, client trust funds are excluded from the firm's assets, contingency-fee revenue is not recognized until the case concludes, and many firms defer recognizing unbilled time to avoid overstating income.

These practices demonstrate how industry norms influence financial reporting, even when they diverge from generally accepted accounting principles.

Legal Angle: In disputes, one party may claim that financial statements deviate from standard GAAP or IFRS, while the other defends the treatment as aligned with accepted industry practices. Understanding these exceptions helps attorneys determine whether a reporting approach is acceptable or deceptive.

4 Why These Matter for Attorneys

Accounting principles, assumptions, and constraints are far more than abstract technicalities. They shape how financial information appears in the very disputes, negotiations, due diligence, and transactions that attorneys handle.

Mastering these fundamentals enables attorneys to:

Spot aggressive or questionable accounting practices.

Ask sharper questions during litigation, arbitration, or M&A due diligence or negotiations.

Strengthen arguments that hinge on financial data (e.g., damages claims, insolvency proceedings, valuation disputes).

For attorneys, understanding the framework behind the numbers is not optional. It is a tool of advocacy, risk management, and professional credibility.

Key Takeaways

Key Takeaways

- Principles = rules, assumptions = ground rules, constraints = limits.
- GAAP and IFRS dominate global reporting; know which applies to your case.
- Industry practices may override GAAP/IFRS, but can be challenged in disputes.
- Violations typically lie at the center of fraud, disputes, or litigation.
- Attorneys should ask: Which assumptions are valid? Which constraints justify exceptions?
- Mastery of these fundamentals strengthens due diligence, litigation strategies, and contract negotiations.

Segue

Understanding the framework is step one. But rules on paper only matter if you can see their impact in practice. That is precisely what we will do when we turn to the financial statements in the following chapters, starting with the Balance Sheet.

5 Exercises

5.1 Identify the Principle

A law firm invoices $50,000 in December, paid in January. Which principle governs the recognition of this revenue?

5.2 Going Concern Violation

A company facing liquidation reports assets at full purchase price. Which assumption is broken? What legal implications arise?

5.3 Cost–Benefit Argument

In litigation, one side claims disclosure of specific client data was too costly. How would you analyze this under the Cost–Benefit constraint?

3 THE BALANCE SHEET — YOUR FINANCIAL SNAPSHOT

Going back to the email that arrived at 11:42 p.m., with the closing set at 9 a.m. the next day. The email just said, "see attached for closing" and included a file titled: "balance sheet."

Instead of the routine tidy-up that I expected, the balance sheet showed a number in the current liabilities line that tripled the one reviewed the day before. My pulse quickened. I felt my stomach tighten. The ticking of the clock echoed on the empty conference room walls, amplifying the sudden dread: Had I missed something crucial? This was not mere numbers on a sheet; it was my professional credibility hanging by a thread

My phone lit up. "Do we walk away?" the junior partner whispered, voice shaking. Silence hung between us. I steadied myself, inhaled sharply, and replied with deliberate calm, "Give me five minutes with the numbers." Those five minutes spent combing a single sheet saved our client seven figures, and perhaps our careers.

Five Minutes to Save the Deal...

As Warren Buffett famously observed, accounting is "the language of business," adding that "unless you are willing to put the effort to learn how to read and interpret financial statements, you really shouldn't select stocks yourself."

We might add that you shouldn't expect to become a successful business lawyer either.

Understanding accounting is essential for assessing financial exposure in deals and disputes, interacting effectively with CEOs, CFOs, auditors, and boards, as well as your own law firm's or company's performance.

Chapter Thesis

The balance sheet reveals what a business owns, what it owes, and what remains for its owners at a single point in time, all **in one snapshot**.

For lawyers, the balance sheet is key in determining if an entity is insolvent or hides liabilities, to negotiate deals, and safeguard client interests. Understanding how the balance sheet works enables lawyers to decipher financial strength, identify potential red flags, and help clients understand and manage associated risks.

Chapter Snapshot – Balance Sheet

Chapter Essentials

- **Snapshot:** Assets = Liabilities + Equity at a given moment.

- **Why it matters:** Basis for solvency, collateral, and working capital definitions.

- **Legal relevance:** Crucial in M&A, bankruptcy, covenant drafting, and partnership disputes.

- **Red flag:** Sudden swings in liabilities or unexplained equity shifts typically indicate manipulation.

Not a Precise Science

Many attorneys are surprised to learn that accounting is not a precise, mathematical language; it is, in fact, subject to interpretation. And we attorneys, of course, are comfortable with interpretation!

This chapter introduces the system that underpins modern accounting. Luca Pacioli, a Renaissance friar, first codified double-entry bookkeeping in 1494. Five centuries later, its core concepts remain unchanged.

A One-Pager

On a single page, the balance sheet reveals what a business owns, what it owes, and the residual value (or risk) for its owners, at a particular moment in time.

Mastering this statement enables lawyers to assess solvency, spot hidden liabilities, negotiate from a position of strength, and safeguard their own firms and clients, all before the first cup of coffee is brewed.

1 The Balance Sheet Equation

At its core, accounting rests on one relationship:

Assets = Liabilities + Equity

Balance Sheet Formula. Assets

Assets = LIABILITIES + OWNER'S EQUITY

Shows that every asset is financed by owners or creditors

Figure 2.1: Balance Sheet Formula. Assets

The balance sheet formula is one of the few formulas you should learn by heart.

Every entry in **double-entry bookkeeping** maintains this equation in balance because **it is recorded on both sides** of the balance sheet (once on each side) **or twice on the same side** (once as a positive number and once as a negative number). The symmetry acts as a built-in error detector.

This fundamental equation is not only accounting theory; it's your fraud detection system. Every manipulation leaves a trail because the books must balance.

We will see how this plays out in practice with a simple law firm example.

Mini case: ABC Law LLP's Opening Day

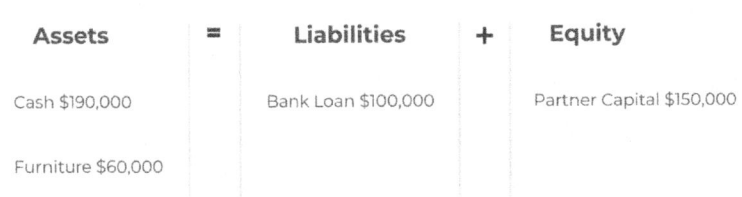

Figure 2.2: ABC Law LLP's Opening Day Balance Sheet

One transaction touches two sides, yet the totals still match. That symmetry is your built-in error detector: Follow the counter-entry, and you follow the money.

This mathematical discipline is the lawyer's first safeguard: Any figure that upsets the balance must have a partner figure somewhere else.

To see the **double-entry bookkeeping more clearly**, we will review the transactions of ABC Law LLP on its opening day.

Figure 2.3: ABC Law LLP's Opening Day Transaction 1

1.1 The Partner capital contribution of $150,000: As you can see, the Partner Capital contribution of $150,000 was recorded first on the right side of the balance sheet, under Equity → Partner Capital. Then, a second entry for the same amount was recorded on the left side of the balance sheet, under Assets → Cash.

The above records mean that the partners of ABC Law LLP contributed $150,000 in cash. If the partners had made the contribution in kind, an entry would still be recorded on the left side, under Assets, but not as cash. We will review how Assets are typically classified on the left side of a balance sheet.

Figure 2.4: ABC Law LLP's Opening Day Transaction 2

1.2 The Bank Loan of $100,000: ABC Law LLP obtained a five-year bank loan for $100,000 to initiate its operations. As you can see, the amount of $100,000 was recorded first on the right side of the balance sheet, under Liabilities → Bank Loan. Then, a second entry for $100,000 was recorded (added to) on the left side of the balance sheet, under Assets → Cash.

Figure 2.5: ABC Law LLP's Opening Day Transaction 3

1.3 The Purchase of Furniture and Tech: Finally, as ABC Law LLP used $60,000 of the loan to purchase office furniture and tech, an entry is made on the left side of the balance sheet, under Assets → Cash, to subtract that amount. Then, an entry is made for the same amount of

$60,000 also on the left side of the balance sheet, under Assets → Furniture, to reflect that $60,000 of cash has been transformed into $60,000 of furniture and tech. Thus, the total amount of Assets remains the same.

Figure 2.6: A Balance Sheet in balance

The ABC Law example illustrates the basics, but real legal work requires understanding what each number means and where companies usually conceal problems. Here is a breakdown of the three main categories that comprise every balance sheet.

What the Balance Sheet Tells You (and Why Lawyers Care)

The balance sheet answers **four critical questions** every lawyer needs to know:

Can they pay? Whether a company has sufficient assets to pay its debts is crucial before advising on litigation or extending credit.

Should you sue? Whether pursuing a debt recovery action makes financial sense, given the debtor's asset position.

Is there value left? Whether owners retain meaningful equity after obligations is essential for partnership disputes and valuations.

Are those shares worth anything? Whether equity offered as collateral or compensation has real value backing it.

More generally, understanding the balance sheet is crucial in various legal contexts, including mergers and acquisitions (M&A) transactions, litigation damages and valuations, partnership compensation and profit-sharing arrangements, loan covenants, financial ratios, corporate governance, and fiduciary duties.

For law firms specifically, it helps assess the firm's financial health, understand liquidity and potential insolvency, and analyze partner buy-ins and exits.

Decoding the Three Headings

Figure 2.7: A Simple Balance Sheet

2 Assets — The Economic Resources

ABC Law LLP's first transactions are simple: Partners contribute $150,000 in cash as equity, the firm receives a loan of $100,000, and it purchases $60,000 of furniture and tech. Over time, ABC Law will add work-in-progress (unbilled hours), accounts receivable (billed but unpaid fees), and perhaps a trademark for a legal-tech product.

Assets represent economic resources that a firm: **(i) owns or controls, (ii) acquired in a transaction, and (iii) which are expected to generate future benefits**. They are recorded at their **historical cost** (i.e., what you paid, as shown in our example).

While modern accounting has shifted toward using **"fair value"** for specific items (e.g., financial instruments), valuing them at what they could be sold for today in the open market rather than their original acquisition price, the balance sheet still has significant limitations as a tool for determining the true value of a business. This is because some of the most valuable aspects of a business do not meet these accounting criteria to qualify as assets.

For example, consider the corporate team that a law firm has built organically over the years through hiring, training, and internal development. This team may be very valuable due to its talent and experience. Still, this value is not listed in the balance sheet as an asset because it wasn't acquired through a specific transaction (such as the acquisition of another law firm). Therefore, there is no reliable historical cost to assign to it. Instead, this kind of value only gets recognized indirectly, perhaps in an M&A transaction if factored into **goodwill**.

Accountants generally classify assets into types. These include:

Current assets: Cash or resources convertible to cash within a year *signal liquidity*.

Examples include cash, marketable securities held as short-term investments, notes receivable, accounts receivable (amounts owed to the firm for goods or services sold on credit), inventories, and prepaid expenses (such as insurance paid in advance).

For law or service firms, this typically includes cash, accounts receivable (fees billed but not collected), client costs advanced (costs paid for clients to be reimbursed), and prepaid expenses.

Non-current/long-term assets: Resources not expected to convert to cash or be used within one year.

Examples include assets used to produce the firm's products or services, referred to as "property, plant, and equipment" (see more below); stocks and bonds intended to be held for the long term; receivables that have been uncollectible for over a year; and long-term prepaid expenses.

Fixed assets - Tangible (Property, Plant, and Equipment): Tangible resources acquired for extended business use, such as land, buildings, machinery, furniture, and fixtures. For law or service firms, this may include office buildings and computer equipment.

Fixed assets - Intangible: Assets that lack physical substance but are acquired for long-term use, such as software, patents, copyrights, and trademarks.

Depreciation & Amortization on the Balance Sheet

Fixed and intangible assets are recorded at historical cost, then reduced by accumulated depreciation (for tangibles) or amortization (for intangibles).

Example: A firm buys $100,000 of equipment with a 10-year useful life. Each year, $10,000 depreciation reduces the asset's book value, so after five years, the balance sheet shows $50,000 (net of accumulated depreciation).

Lawyer Application

- Overstating asset values (by under-depreciating) inflates equity and misleads creditors or investors.

- In partner disputes or M&A deals, disagreements many times arise over whether goodwill and intangibles are properly amortized.

- In insolvency, artificially high asset values may give a false impression of solvency.

- Always check accumulated depreciation/amortization schedules to test whether assets are fairly valued.

Liquidity Shelve

Figure 2.8: Liquidity Shelve

Accountants usually list current assets first and in order of how easily and quickly they can be converted into cash (easier and quicker first), which makes it easier for creditors to assess the company's cash position. They follow with non-current assets, fixed assets, and intangible assets, in that order.

Quick reference: Typical law-firm assets

- **Current:** Cash, fee receivables, client costs advanced, prepaid insurance.

- **Long-term:** Security deposits, strategic equity stakes.

- **Property & equipment:** Leasehold improvements, computers, equipment.

- **Intangibles:** Proprietary document-automation software, trade name, CLE content library.

Figures 2.9 and 2.10 are an extract from the asset section of two well-known international law firms, which show the types of assets listed.

CLIFFORD
CHANCE

FINANCIAL STATEMENTS
FOR THE YEAR ENDED 30 APRIL 2021

CONSOLIDATED BALANCE SHEET

As at 30 April	Note	2021 £m	2020 £m
ASSETS			
Property, plant and equipment	12	72	77
Right of use assets	26	311	334
Finance lease receivable – non-current	26	120	145
Deferred tax asset	10	51	55
Total Non-Current Assets		554	611
Accrued income	25	305	295
Trade and other receivables	14	457	506
Finance lease receivable – current	26	23	23
Amounts due from members	15	88	79
Cash and cash equivalents	16	370	299
Total Current Assets		1,243	1,202
TOTAL ASSETS		1,797	1,813

Figure 2.9: Clifford Chance Consolidated Balance Sheet. Assets

Consolidated balance sheet

	Notes	At 30 April 2024 £'m	At 30 April 2023 £'m
Assets			
Non-current assets			
Property, plant and equipment	10	84.4	75.9
Right-of-use assets	12	480.2	276.3
Intangible assets	14	14.0	10.8
Investments	15	0.1	0.1
Deferred tax asset	17	–	1.7
		578.7	364.8
Current assets			
Trade and other receivables	16	994.2	865.1
Amounts due from members	21	111.8	81.0
Cash and cash equivalents	18	184.7	202.8
		1,290.7	1,148.9
Total assets		**1,869.4**	**1,513.7**

Figure 2.10: Linklaters LLP Consolidated Balance Sheet. Assets

---

Lawyer Application

When you are conducting due diligence for mergers or acquisitions, carefully verify the fair valuation of intangible assets, such as trademarks or proprietary technology. Note that inflated valuations here can conceal negative tangible net worth, creating unforeseen liabilities for your client.

 MALPRACTICE ALERT: The Unearned-Retainer Trap

Client retainers aren't your money until you earn them. These funds should be recorded as liabilities until the work is performed. Mixing unearned retainers with operating cash can violate trust-account rules and void malpractice coverage. Always record "Unearned Retainer Fees" in the current-liability column and track the matching work-in-progress entry that will earn them.

Key Takeaways

Assets — Key Takeaways

- Assets represent resources generating future economic benefit.
- Verify asset valuations, in particular "fair value", and intangible assets valuation.

This leads us to the second component of the balance sheet.

3 Liabilities — The Obligations

Liabilities are obligations to pay. They originate in contracts, torts, or the passage of time (i.e., interest). To be recognized in the balance sheet, they generally must be: (i) present or current; (ii) stemming from a prior transaction or occurrence, not a future one; (iii) their settlement will likely require an outflow of economic resources from the firm, and (iv) the amount must be reasonably quantified.

The balance sheet does not capture some of the most **significant negative value** aspects of a business that do not meet this accounting criteria to qualify as liabilities (e.g., bad management, poor morale, bad reputation), thereby adding significant limitations to the balance sheet as a tool for determining the true value of a business.

In the case of ABC Law, it finances part of its fit-out with a bank loan. It also holds client retainers that must remain untouched until earned, a fact that many lawyers overlook when they treat those funds as operating cash. The retainer is a liability: An IOU to the client until the work is done.

Balance Sheet Formula. Liabilities

$$\text{Liabilities} = \text{ASSETS} - \text{OWNER'S EQUITY}$$

Shows the portion of assets financed with debt

Figure 2.11: Balance Sheet Formula. Liabilities

Liabilities are categorized into:

Current liabilities: (due within a year).

Typically includes accounts payable (amounts owed to suppliers for goods purchased on credit), accrued liabilities or wages (expenses incurred for services performed but not yet paid), short-term debt or notes (due within one year), and any portion of long-term debt due within one year.

For law firms, this includes accounts payable and unearned retainer fees (retainers received from clients for work not yet performed).

Non-current liabilities: (due to mature later).

Examples include long-term loans or bonds payable, less the portion that is due within the current period.

Finally, liabilities are generally listed in descending order of maturity (when they are due).

Lawyer Application

When drafting loan agreements or covenants, try to precisely define which obligations fall under the category of "current liabilities." Imprecision can allow counterparties to shift long-term liabilities into current ones at critical moments, potentially triggering covenant breaches.

For example, a balloon payment that is classified as a current liability can greatly affect a financial ratio and trigger default overnight. See subchapter 5 below discussing ratios.

 MALPRACTICE ALERT: Covenant Ambiguity

Attorneys drafting ambiguous loan covenants that can facilitate manipulations could be exposed to malpractice claims. Always specify precise financial metrics.

Key Takeaways

Liabilities — Key Takeaways

- Liabilities represent obligations owed to others. Closely monitor short-term obligations.
- Clearly define liabilities in loan covenants to avoid unexpected defaults.
- Remember that client retainers are liabilities until earned. Safeguard your ethical obligations.

4 Equity — The Residual Claim (Net Worth)

Balance Sheet Formula. Owner's Equity

Owner's Equity = ASSETS − LIABILITY

Highlights the owners' residual stake

Figure 2.12: Balance Sheet Formula. Owner's Equity

Equity is what remains after deducting liabilities from assets.

On a legal firm's balance sheet, on day 1, equity equals the partners' capital contributions. Equity will later expand with further partner contributions and with retained profits, and it will contract with losses, distributions, and capital withdrawals.

ABC Law LLP's Month-end Equity Snapshot

Partner Capital	$150,000
Retained Earnings (Current Month)	+ $5,000
Cash Draws	− $3,000
Total Equity	$152,000

A single profit month increases equity; partner draws immediately reduces it.

Figure 2.13: Month-end Equity Snapshot for ABC Law LLP

Lawyer Application

In partner buy-in negotiations, explicitly clarify how intangible assets, such as goodwill, are valued. Failure to do so may result in disputes if future impairments occur, which could drastically affect equity and lead to costly partnership conflicts.

 MALPRACTICE ALERT: Partner Equity Wrong Valuation

Goodwill or intangible assets inflated without adequate justification in partner equity calculations can trigger serious partnership disputes and malpractice risks.

Key Takeaways

Equity — Key Takeaways

- Equity reflects residual claims by owners after debts are paid.
- Monitor partner capital accounts closely; goodwill impairments affect partners' equity.
- Ensure equity adjustments in deals are explicitly outlined to avoid valuation disputes.

ABC Law gets to work

As ABC Law gets into business, the balance sheet reflects new transactions. As shown in Figure 2.14, with its capital structure, the firm has transformed or produced new assets (accounts receivable, work-in-progress, and prepaid expenses), increased its bank loan balance, and owner's equity.

Specifically, note that in Assets → Cash started at $190,000 and is now $100,000, while Furniture remains at $60,000. However, there are now $115,000 in Accounts Receivable, $40,000 in Work-in-Progress, and $5,000 in Prepaid Expenses. In total, Assets increased from $250,000 to $320,000, representing a $70,000 rise.

How was this financed? ABC Law had to purchase certain inputs that it had not yet paid for. They appear under Liabilities, in a new entry titled "Accounts Payable" for $30,000. Additionally, the Bank Loan initially started at $100,000 and has since increased to $138,000, indicating that the firm has received additional funds to cover operational expenses that have already been paid (i.e., not reflected as liabilities). In total, Liabilities increased from $100,000 to $168,000, a rise of $68,000.

In the meantime, Equity increased from $150,000 to $152,000. This means that at the time of this balance sheet photo, the Firm was able to produce a surplus from its operations, which increased the owners' claim in it. To know how this happened, refer to the Month-end Equity Snapshot, Figure 2.13 in this same chapter, where you will also be surprised to find a $3,000 draw paid to partners that is not explicitly captured in the balance sheet. This indicates that the balance sheet does not provide the full story, and you should also review the other financial statements designed to give you additional information.

To make sure that everything is in order, confirm that the balance sheet equation balances:

Assets ($320,000) = Liabilities ($168,000) + Equity ($152,000)

The Balance sheet is in balance: $320,000 = $320,000

ABC Law LLP's Balance Sheet

Assets	Liabilities
Cash $100,000	Acc Payable $30,000
Acc Recievable $115,000	
WIP* $40,000	Bank Loan $138,000
Furniture $60,000	**Equity**
Prepaid Exp $5,000	$152,000

* Work in Progress

Figure 2.14: ABC Law LLP's Balance Sheet

5 Financial Ratios from the Balance Sheet

Financial ratios derived from the balance sheet are used when drafting or negotiating contracts, such as loan agreements and asset-based deals, as well as when evaluating business transactions. These ratios can assess liquidity (the ability to meet short-term obligations) and solvency (the ability to meet long-term obligations). Therefore, it is critical for a business lawyer to understand these ratios.

Examples include the current ratio (Current Assets / Current Liabilities) and the debt-to-equity ratio (Total Liabilities / Equity).

It's important to remember that these ratios can only be trusted if the balance sheet figures from which they are computed are reliable. If assets or liabilities are misstated, the ratios will be misleading. If you include ratios in a legal agreement, try to define with precision how they will be calculated.

Additonally, the ratios mentioned in the book are a general guideline. For more specific insights contrast them with the ratios of comparable competitors in the specific industry.

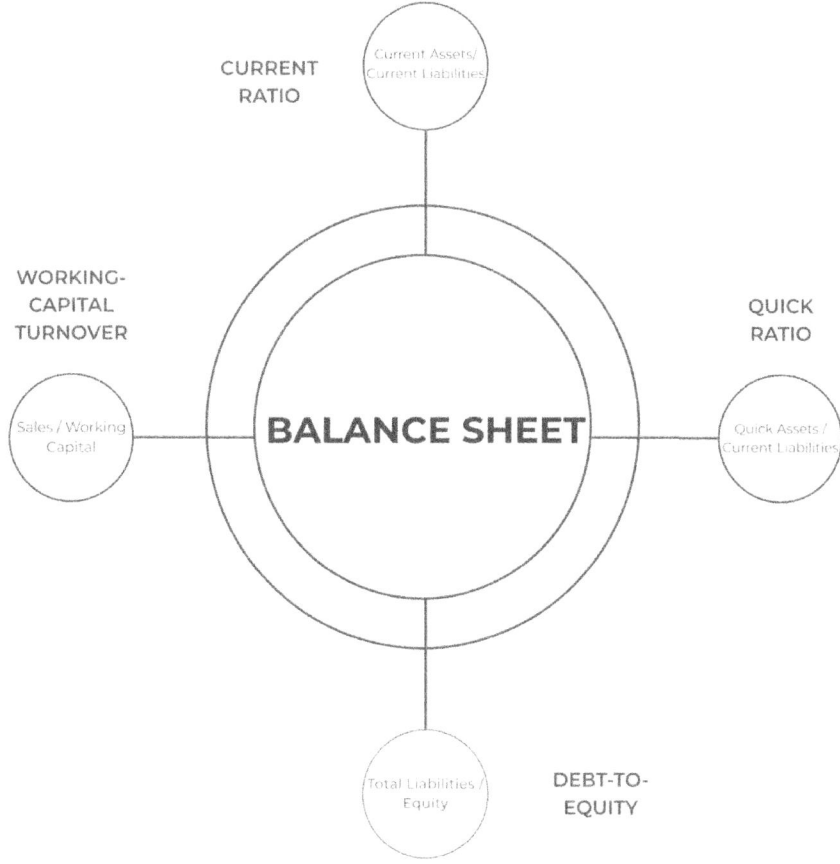

Figure 2.15: Balance Sheet Ratios

The Five-Minute Financial Health Check:

- **Liquidity Test (current ratio)**: Current Assets ÷ Current Liabilities. A ratio below 1.0 signals a potential cash crunch. Note that 1.0 is a minimum, not necessarily a healthy ratio.

- **Leverage Check (debt-to-equity)**: Total Debt ÷ Equity.

Above 3:1? High leverage can wipe out your client's stake if earnings falter.

- **Maturity Mismatch**: Long-term assets funded by short-term debt? Cash flow nightmare ahead.

- **Covenant Precision**: Never accept vague terms. Demand exact definitions: "Current Assets excluding work-in-progress valued above $X."

- **Footnote Mining**: Examine carefully the notes. A short sentence about "other receivables" can reveal millions in uncollectible debt.

Key Takeaways

Financial Ratios — Key Takeaways

- Always confirm the accuracy of balance sheet figures used in ratio calculations.
- Precise ratio definitions are critical; ambiguity leads to disputes and manipulation risks.
- Ratios can be powerful negotiation tools for drafting robust contractual covenants.

Lawyer's Tip

Due diligence red flags: Essential ratios to calculate immediately:

- Current ratio <1.0 = cash crisis looming
- Debt-to-equity >3:1 = owners' stake vulnerable
- Working capital trending negative = insolvency risk

Documents to demand: 3+ years of monthly balance sheets, not just year-end

6 Beyond the Face: Notes, Audits, and Management Discussion & Analysis (MD&A)

The balance sheet is only the cover page. The **Notes** disclose accounting policies, contingencies, and off-balance-sheet commitments, and they also give context to material accounting entries.

The **auditor's opinion** tells you whether to trust the numbers, and the **MD&A** offers management's (unaudited) spin. Seasoned lawyers read all three before negotiating or litigating anything financial.

Look, for instance, at non-current liabilities in the Linklaters LLP consolidated balance sheet. You will notice a significant increase in non-current lease liabilities, which jumped from (258.3) in 2023 to (501.9) in 2024. To understand the reason for that change, you will need to read the relevant Note (Note 12). The lack of a note would be a warning sign.

Current liabilities			
Trade and other payables	19	(520.3)	(454.9)
Lease liabilities	12	(37.1)	(57.9)
Current tax liabilities		(11.3)	(15.7)
Provisions	20	(17.1)	(1.7)
Members' capital classified as a liability	21	(71.0)	(72.7)
		(656.8)	(602.9)
Non-current liabilities			
Provisions	20	(28.7)	(57.1)
Lease liabilities	12	(501.9)	(258.3)
Post-retirement benefits	24	(0.4)	(0.3)
Members' capital classified as a liability	21	(54.0)	(48.3)
Deferred tax liability	17	(1.5)	–
		(586.5)	(364.0)

Figure 2.16: Linklaters LLP Consolidated Balance Sheet. Liabilities

Note 12 (Lease liabilities): By reading this note, you will learn that the increase in non-current lease liabilities relates to the lease of the new head office in London, which became effective 29 days before the closing of the 2024 economic period.

Additions to the right-of-use assets during the year ended 30 April 2024 were £263.5m (2023: £36.7m). Within these additions is £216.8m relating to the new London head office, 20 Ropemaker Street, which lease commenced on 1 April 2024.

Lease liabilities	30 April 2024 £'m	30 April 2023 £'m
Current	37.1	57.9
Non-current	501.9	258.3
	539.0	316.2

Figure 2.17: Linklaters LLP Consolidated Balance Sheet. Note 12

However, upon examining the management discussion and analysis, you will notice that the firm plans to relocate to its new headquarters in 2026, despite the lease becoming effective on April 1, 2024, which may raise questions about the specific terms of the lease and the firm's cost management.

Premises

The firm's office selection criteria include assessing the potential climate risks and opportunities associated with different buildings. Where available, the firm aims to target environmentally accredited buildings and for the designs and fit-outs of those buildings to reflect the firm's sustainability and environmental policies outlined in its Global Design Guide and Sustainable Design Checklists. For example, from 2026 the firm's headquarters will relocate to a new office in London (20 Ropemaker). That building and its fit-out are designed to be BREEAM "Outstanding" rated and WELL "Platinum" certified, and the core base build has been awarded an EPC A rating. The firm uses such standards to ensure that it meets its commitment to sustainable development as well as to help mitigate against the physical risk identified above of the firm's people, offices and/or operations being impacted by climate change.

7 Balance Sheet Red-Flag Checklist for Lawyers

The 60-Second Fraud Detector

- Current liabilities > current assets (liquidity crisis)
- Sudden changes in asset categories (manipulation?)
- Large "other" line items without explanation
- Working capital declining for 2+ consecutive periods
- Debt-to-equity ratio increasing rapidly
- Goodwill/Intangible Bloat - Asset quality issue

Figure 2.18: The 60-Second Fraud Detector

Subchapter 7 presents a concise checklist of balance sheet red flags that lawyers should be aware of when reviewing a company's financial statements. These warnings typically signal potential accounting manipulations, liquidity crises, or unsustainable practices that can end in disputes, regulatory investigations, or breaches of fiduciary duty.

For lawyers involved in litigation, due diligence, or contract negotiations, recognizing these red flags is key to identifying risks that could impact solvency opinions, covenant compliance, valuation disputes, or allegations of fraud.

Current Liabilities > Current Assets (Liquidity Crisis Looming)

This red flag appears when current liabilities exceed current assets, resulting in a current ratio below 1.0. It warns that the company cannot pay its short-term obligations with readily available assets, signaling an immediate liquidity emergency.

For example, a company with $800,000 in current assets but $1,000,000 in current liabilities faces a $200,000 shortfall that must be resolved in the short term (within 12 months). This situation can trigger a cascade of legal problems, including supplier demands for cash payments, employee concerns about payroll, and lender covenant violations. In bankruptcy contexts, this can serve as evidence of insolvency, making recent payments to creditors potentially recoverable as preferences.

Lawyers who understand the situation are capable of investigating whether management has a feasible plan to address the shortfall and whether continued operations constitute a breach of fiduciary duties to creditors.

Lawyer's Tip

Liquidity crisis investigation: Key documents to examine:
- Weekly cash flow projections vs. actual
- Accounts payable aging reports
- Supplier payment terms and extension letters
- Board minutes discussing cash management

- Sudden Liability Reclassifications Without Business Justification

This red flag involves significant shifts between liability categories that appear to be designed to manipulate financial ratios rather than reflect genuine business changes. Companies may reclassify current liabilities as long-term to improve their current ratio or move operating expenses to the balance sheet as "assets" to inflate profits.

For instance, a company struggling with covenant compliance might reclassify $2 million of current liabilities as "long-term debt" just before quarter-end, artificially improving its current ratio. While some reclassifications reflect legitimate business changes, those occurring near financial reporting deadlines or covenant testing dates warrant scrutiny. This manipulation can mislead lenders about liquidity, distort acquisition valuations, and trigger audit investigations.

Lawyers should examine whether these changes follow appropriate approval processes and whether they comply with accounting standards, as improper reclassifications can lead to restatements, covenant breaches, and regulatory enforcement actions.

Lawyer's Tip

Asset manipulation detection: Essential discovery requests:

- Monthly balance sheet rollforwards showing reclassifications
- Asset capitalization policy changes and board approvals
- External auditor management letters questioning classifications

Investigation focus: Any reclassification >10% of total assets Internal emails discussing "balance sheet management"

- Large or Growing "Other" Line Items Without Explanation

Be careful with "Other Assets" or "Other Liabilities" categories.

"Other" categories should typically represent less than 5% of total assets or liabilities; when they exceed this threshold or grow rapidly without clear footnote disclosure, they often conceal related-party transactions, contingent liabilities, or off-balance-sheet commitments that have migrated onto the balance sheet.

For example, a company might park $10 million of loans to executives in "Other Assets" to avoid prominent disclosure or bury environmental cleanup obligations in "Other Liabilities" to minimize investor attention. These catch-all categories can conceal self-dealing transactions from auditors, obscure the true extent of a company's obligations, and violate disclosure requirements for public companies.

Lawyers should demand detailed supporting schedules for any significant "other" balances, as they often contain the smoking guns in fraud investigations and the hidden liabilities that can derail transactions.

Lawyer's Tip

"Other" category investigation: Target documents for review:

- Detailed general ledger supporting "other" balances
- Related-party transaction agreements and approvals
- Contingent liability analysis and legal reserves
- Asset retirement obligation schedules

Smoking gun: "Other" items >5% of total assets without clear explanation

---

- Working Capital Declining for Multiple Consecutive Periods

This red flag occurs when working capital (current assets minus current liabilities) deteriorates over successive quarters, indicating the company is consuming cash faster than it generates it from operations. Declining working capital often reflects slowing collections from customers, building inventory that isn't selling, or accelerated payments to suppliers who have tightened credit terms.

For instance, a manufacturing company whose working capital drops from $5 million to $3 million to $1 million over consecutive quarters is clearly heading toward a liquidity crisis. This trend often precedes formal insolvency and can trigger going-concern qualifications from auditors, making the company vulnerable to preference payment claims in the event of bankruptcy. The decline may also indicate management's awareness of impending financial distress, which can lead to director liability claims if they continue operations while insolvent.

Lawyers should analyze whether the decline in working capital stems from operational issues, collection problems, or deliberate cash management strategies that may constitute preferential treatment of certain creditors.

Lawyer's Tip

Working capital deterioration analysis: Critical evidence to obtain:

- Monthly working capital trend analysis by component
- Customer concentration reports and collection statistics
- Inventory turnover analysis and obsolescence reserves
- Management projections vs. actual working capital performance

Legal trigger: Working capital negative or declining >25% year-over-year

---

- Debt Maturity Wall: Large Long-Term Debt Becoming Current

This situation happens when significant portions of long-term debt are scheduled to mature in the short term (within the next 12 months), creating a "maturity wall" that must be refinanced or repaid. When more than 30% of total debt becomes current, the company faces substantial refinancing risk, particularly if credit markets tighten or the company's financial condition deteriorates.

For example, a company with $20 million in total debt might see $8 million shift from long-term to current liabilities as a bond issue approaches maturity, which would immediately worsen all liquidity ratios and potentially trigger covenant violations. This situation often leads to expensive refinancing terms, requires complex workout negotiations, or forces companies into *Chapter 11* reorganization to extend debt maturities.

The maturity wall problem can trigger cross-default provisions in other debt agreements, create lender disputes over workout terms versus foreclosure rights, and expose recent payments to maturing creditors as potential preferences.

Lawyers should carefully analyze debt maturity schedules, as companies may attempt to minimize the disclosure of near-term refinancing risks until they become unavoidable.

Lawyer's Tip

- Debt maturity analysis: Must-have evidence:
- Debt maturity schedules by instrument and lender
- Credit facility utilization reports and availability
- Covenant compliance certificates and waiver requests
- Management correspondence with lenders about refinancing

Danger zone: >30% of total debt maturing within 12 months

- Goodwill and Intangible Assets > 40% of Total Assets

This warning sign indicates that a company's balance sheet is heavily weighted toward intangible assets, which may have little value in the event of liquidation. Goodwill and intangible assets typically result from overpriced acquisitions (claimed to be for "strategic reasons") and are subject to impairment when business conditions deteriorate. When these assets exceed 40% of the total asset base, the company faces significant impairment risk and lacks tangible asset coverage for its obligations.

For instance, a technology company with $100 million in total assets might carry $60 million in goodwill from acquisitions, leaving only $40 million in tangible assets to support $80 million in liabilities; a recipe for insolvency if the goodwill must be written down. High intangible asset concentrations create problems in solvency analyses, as these assets typically have minimal liquidation value, making it difficult to argue that creditors would be paid in full if the company were to be forced into liquidation. This imbalance often leads to disputes over asset valuations in M&A transactions, impairment charges that trigger covenant violations, and challenges in bankruptcy proceedings where courts and creditors heavily discount intangible asset values.

Lawyer's Tip

Intangible asset investigation: Key documents to analyze:

- Purchase price allocation reports from acquisitions
- Annual impairment testing work papers and assumptions
- Independent valuation reports for intangible assets
- Management projections supporting asset values

Red flag threshold: Goodwill >50% of equity or declining business performance

---

- The Ultimate Danger Signal: Negative Tangible Net Worth

This is the most significant red flag on any balance sheet and indicates technical insolvency when measured only by tangible assets. When a company's tangible net worth becomes negative, it means that if forced to liquidate using only hard assets (cash, inventory, equipment, real estate), creditors would not receive full payment even if every tangible asset was sold for its book value. This calculation removes the accounting fiction of goodwill, patents, and other intangibles that often hold little or no value in liquidation scenarios.

For example, a company with $50 million in total assets might seem solvent, but if $40 million is goodwill from acquisitions and total liabilities are $45 million, the tangible net worth is negative $35 million—a severe insolvency that goodwill hides. This situation creates immediate legal risks on multiple levels: recent payments to creditors could be challenged as preferences in bankruptcy, directors could face personal liability for continuing operations while technically insolvent, and any new obligations might be considered fraudulent transfers.

Courts focus on tangible net worth in solvency analyses because it represents the harsh reality of liquidation value, making this metric particularly crucial in preference litigation, fraudulent transfer claims, and director liability cases where the timing of insolvency determines legal exposure.

(Total Assets — Intangible Assets) — Total Liabilities < 0

Figure 2.19: Negative Tangible Net Worth Red Flag

Essential Discovery Roadmap

Whether you've identified one red flag or multiple warning signs, systematic document discovery is fundamental for building your case or safeguarding your client. Start by requesting monthly balance sheets for at least 24 months instead of relying on year-end snapshots, which can hide quarterly fluctuations and manipulations.

Simultaneously, demand the detailed general ledger supporting major balance sheet accounts, as this reveals the actual transactions behind summary numbers. Debt agreements and their amendment history are crucial for understanding covenant calculations and waiver negotiations that may indicate financial distress.

Asset appraisals and impairment analyses expose whether companies are carrying assets at unrealistic values, while related-party transaction schedules can reveal self-dealing that distorts the balance sheet.

In follow-up discovery, focus on cash-flow projections versus actual performance to demonstrate management's awareness of problems.

Additionally, review board minutes discussing the financial condition to identify potential breaches of fiduciary duty. External auditor management letters and recommendations frequently contain the most damaging admissions about accounting irregularities and internal control failures, making them very valuable in fraud cases.

This systematic approach ensures you capture both the smoking guns and the material evidence needed for complex financial litigation.

The 5-Minute Diagnostic Protocol

Comprehensive discovery takes time, but you often need answers immediately, such as during a client call, in the middle of due diligence, or when reviewing documents at 11 p.m.

Here's your rapid-fire diagnostic protocol for assessing balance sheet health in real-time: a practical tool for lawyers navigating balance sheet complexities.

The 5-Minute Diagnostic Protocol

When reviewing any balance sheet, follow this sequence:

Step 1: Calculate current ratio (Current Assets ÷ Current Liabilities)

Step 2: Check working capital trend (Current Assets - Current Liabilities)

Step 3: Analyze debt maturity (How much debt due within 12 months?)

Step 4: Assess asset quality (What % is goodwill/intangibles?)

Step 5: Hunt for "other" categories (Any large unexplained balances?)

If ANY ratio triggers the thresholds above → Investigate immediately

Figure 2.20: The 5-Minute Diagnostic Protocol

8 Connecting to the Other Statements

Profit reported on the income statement flows into **retained earnings** on the balance sheet. The cash-flow statement reconciles book profit with hard cash, revealing whether earnings are solid or built on credit. Viewed together, the three statements form a circuit, break one link, and the numbers stop making sense.

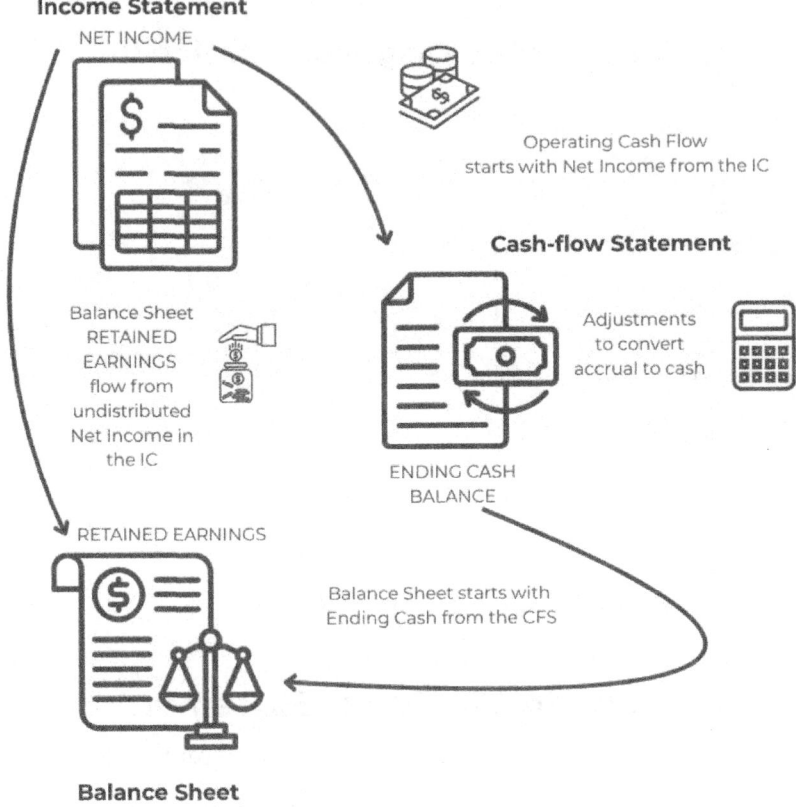

Figure 2.21: Connecting the Financial Statements

9 Stories from the Trenches

- **The 2 a.m. Discovery:** A sudden liability spike in the target's balance sheet led us to discover an undisclosed bridge loan. The seller hadn't disclosed this debt, which violated their representations. Result: $2 million price reduction, additional escrow requirements, and a new repayment covenant that protected our client from hidden debt bombs.

- **The Phantom Partner Buy-In:** A lateral partner paid a hefty buy-in based on book equity that included goodwill booked at whim. Six months later, cash flow stress revealed negative tangible equity *and buyer's remorse.*

- **Preference Litigation:** In bankruptcy court, we demonstrated insolvency on the transfer date by reconstructing net working capital from ledger entries to source documents, thereby turning a routine claw-back case into a full recovery for our client.

- **Retainer-Commingling Fiasco:** A mid-sized firm swept $300,000 of client retainers into its general account to "smooth cash flow." A surprise audit led to immediate repayment and a public reprimand, demonstrating that liabilities ignored on the balance sheet can become ethical grenades.

Key Takeaways

Key Takeaways

- Balance sheet = snapshot of financial position at a moment in time.

- Assets, liabilities, and equity each carry legal risks.
- Ratios derived from the balance sheet inform covenants and negotiations.
- Notes, audits, and MD&A are critical for a comprehensive legal understanding.

Callback

Returning to the opening of this chapter: Review of the amended balance sheet received overnight revealed that a supplier had demanded immediate payment, converting a hidden liability into a ticking financial bomb. By decoding this balance sheet insight, the transaction closed with a price drop.

In the Accounting Principles chapter, we saw that consistency, disclosure, and faithful representation govern the recording of figures. The balance sheet applies those rules to reveal the financial position at a single moment.

Segue

But a snapshot is not the full picture. To understand how performance unfolds across time, we next examine the income statement.

10 Exercises

10.1 Liquidity Check

Current assets = $320,000; current liabilities = $168,000. What is the current ratio? What legal issues arise if it drops below 1.0?

10.2 Equity Dispute

Partners argue about including goodwill in the valuation of equity. How should lawyers address this in a buy-in agreement?

10.3 Red Flag Hunt

A balance sheet shows liabilities tripling overnight without explanation.

As counsel, what steps would you take before approving a deal?

4 THE INCOME STATEMENT — TURNING A YEAR-LONG STORY INTO ONE PAGE OF NUMBERS

It is no coincidence that this situation took place on New Year's Eve. The clock marked 11:40 p.m. exactly when the controller at Digital Components Inc. sent two "rush" invoices, both for $480,000, to a customer we'd never heard of. The address? A P.O. box.

Something didn't add up. I zoomed in on the income statement, where these two invoices conveniently landed just in time to meet a quarterly revenue target and trigger a multi-million-dollar bonus pool.

A few days later, in the new fiscal year, both invoices vanished, replaced by credit memos, but not before the bonuses had been paid and the company had secured new financing. Six months later, those invoices resurfaced in litigation, and the executive team faced clawbacks.

The warning was in plain sight, but no one looked carefully. One headline number, **Revenues**, had concealed a serious misrepresentation.

Income Statement

1. Revenues
2. Expenses
3. Profit or Loss

Figure 3.1: The Income Statement

That Digital Components fraud succeeded because the lawyers reviewing the deal didn't understand the story hidden in plain sight on the income statement. Every financial manipulation leaves fingerprints; you just need to know where to look.

Chapter Thesis

The income statement condenses a year of business activity into a single page, showing how a company generates profit, or the illusion of it. For lawyers, it is a critical tool for analyzing revenue recognition, valuing companies, questioning bonuses, and challenging damage claims. Mastery of the income statement allows you to detect manipulation, ask sharper questions, and see the legal consequences behind every line.

Chapter Snapshot – Income Statement

Chapter Essentials

- **Purpose:** Shows revenues, expenses, and net income over a period.

- **Contrast with balance sheet:** Not a snapshot, but a movie of performance.

- **Legal angle:** Core in damage claims, valuation disputes, and fraud cases.

- **Warning:** Every manipulation leaves fingerprints on this statement.

We will first establish how the income statement fits into the broader financial picture and why *timing* matters more than you might think.

DECEMBER 31

1 What the Income Statement Shows

In the balance sheet chapter, we learned that it is designed to reveal, on a single page, what a business owns, what it owes, and the residual value (or risk) for its owners at a particular moment in time. We also learned that the balance sheet doesn't tell the whole story of a business, and therefore, we need to review other financial statements to fill in the gaps.

The **income statement** (often referred to as the Profit and Loss, or "P&L," or Statement of Earnings or Operations) tells a company's performance story over time, typically covering twelve months of revenues earned and expenses incurred. Unlike the balance sheet's snapshot, which captures assets, liabilities, and equity as of a specific date, this statement reveals whether the business made or lost money over a specified period, usually a full year (e.g., fiscal year).

The result in the income statement, either a profit or a loss, will be recorded in the balance sheet, increasing or reducing the owners' equity accordingly. In the balance sheet chapter, we saw how Retained Earnings increased ABC Law LLP's Equity by $5,000.

The income statement, **on one page**: As a way of introduction, we will review the general concepts of Revenues, Expenses, and Net Income:

1.1 Revenues:

Revenue is the economic benefit obtained by the business from its *ordinary activities* during an accounting or fiscal period. In the case of ABC Law LLP, revenue would be the amount the firm earns from the sale of its legal services. It is key to understand that Revenue is different from Gain.

Gains are an economic benefit obtained by the firm from *incidental or peripheral activities, excluding contributions from owners*. In the case of ABC Law LLP, a profit coming from the sale of foreign currency holdings or furniture would be considered a gain, not revenue.

It is important to notice that Revenues and Gains can increase assets, decrease liabilities, or both, thus increasing owners' equity.

1.2 Expenses:

Expenses are a decrease in economic benefits the business incurs in generating revenue from its *ordinary activities* during an accounting or fiscal period. It is also essential to understand that Expenses are different from Losses.

Losses are a decrease in economic benefit incurred by the firm from *incidental or peripheral activities, excluding distributions to owners.* In the case of ABC Law LLP, a negative result coming from the sale of foreign currency holdings or furniture would be considered a loss, not an expense.

It is also important to keep in mind that Expenses and Losses can decrease assets, increase liabilities, or both, thus reducing owners' equity.

1.3 Net Income:

Net Income is what is left after subtracting all expenses and losses from all revenues and gains during an accounting or fiscal period. It represents an increase or (decrease) in equity, excluding owner contributions and distributions.

Now that we have a general idea of the logic informing the income statement (Revenue – Expenses = Net Income), let's look into it in more detail.

2 Presentation Formats — Single-Step vs. Multi-Step

There is no specific way the income statement should be presented, provided the information is clear and understandable. Having said that, the income statement is generally conveyed in a Single-Step or Multi-Step form.

The Single-Step can be used for small firms and quick analysis, where breaking down the information may not be necessary. In contrast, the multi-step is recommended for larger companies with more complex business operations, where subtotals are required to answer various legal and business questions, and detailed information is fundamental.

Income Statement Formats: What Lawyers Need to Know

Format	Structure	Best For	Legal Implications
Single-Step	All revenues – all expenses = net income	Small private firms; quick analysis	Hides operating performance; less useful for covenant analysis
Multi-Step	Revenue → Gross Profit → Operating Income → EBIT → Net Income	Public companies; detailed analysis	Each subtotal answers different legal questions; preferred for litigation

Figure 3.2: Income Statement Formats: What Lawyers Need to Know

Format matters, and the real power lies in knowing which specific number to focus on for your business or legal issue. Each line on a multi-step income statement tells a different part of a story. It's time to dissect these numbers line by line.

Lawyer's Tip

Format choice tells a story: What to investigate:

- Why switch from multi to single-step? (Often hides declining margins)
- Request 3+ years of internal management reports
- Compare external vs. internal reporting formats
- Look for "adjusted" metrics that exclude normal expenses

Litigation advantage: Multi-step statements provide more ammunition for damages calculations

---

3 The Four Critical Subtotals

We will use The Coca-Cola Company's ("KO") income statement for the fiscal period ending on December 31, 2024, provided in Table 3.1, as an example of a multi-step income statement, and review the critical subtotals every lawyer should understand.

KO / Financials

Coca-Cola Company (The) Common Stock (KO) Financials

Income Statement   Balance Sheet   Cash Flow   Financial Ratios

Period Ending:			12/31/2024	12/31/2023
Total Revenue			$47,061,000	$45,754,000
Cost of Revenue	⟶	COGS	$18,324,000	$18,520,000
Gross Profit			**$28,737,000**	**$27,234,000**
Operating Expenses				
Research and Development			--	--
Sales, General and Admin.			$18,745,000	$15,923,000
Non-Recurring Items			--	--
Other Operating Items			--	--
Operating Income			$9,992,000	$11,311,000
Add'l income/expense items			$2,980,000	$1,477,000
Earnings Before Interest and Tax	⟶	EBIT	$14,742,000	$14,479,000
Interest Expense			$1,656,000	$1,527,000
Earnings Before Tax			$13,086,000	$12,952,000
Income Tax			$2,437,000	$2,249,000
Minority Interest			$1,770,000	$1,691,000
Equity Earnings/Loss Unconsolidated Subsidiary			-$18,000	$11,000
Net Income-Cont. Operations			$12,401,000	$12,405,000
Net Income			**$10,631,000**	**$10,714,000**
Net Income Applicable to Common Shareholders			$10,631,000	$10,714,000

Table 3.1: The Coca-Cola Company (KO) Income Statement

- **Revenue** = Income earned from goods sold or services rendered

KO had a total revenue of $47,061,000.

- **Gross Profit** = Revenue − Cost of Goods Sold (COGS) (or of services rendered)

To produce its revenue, KO incurred direct expenses of $18,324,000.

- **Operating Income (also called Operating Profit)** = Gross Profit − Operating Expenses (e.g., rent, salaries, marketing)

KO spent $18,745,000 in overhead or indirect costs to generate its revenue.

- **EBIT (Earnings Before Interest and Taxes)** = Operating Income ± Non-Operating Income/Expenses (e.g., investment income, one-time gains/losses)

To the Operating Income of $9,992,000, we need to add or subtract income/expenses from *incidental or peripheral activities, excluding contributions from owners*. According to KO's statement, we need to add $2,980,000 for additional income and $1,770,000 for minority interest in other businesses. The total amount is equal to $14,742,000, correctly shown as EBIT.

- **Net Income** = EBIT − Interest − Taxes ± Extraordinary Items

KO's Net Income of $10,631,000 is the result of $14,742,000 (EBIT) - $1,656,000 (Interest Expense) - $2,437,000 (Income Tax) − $18,000.

Let's look in more detail at what each line on a multi-step income statement means and its importance to attorneys with the help of

Figure 3.3.

4 Line-by-Line Walk-Through and Red Flags

LINE-BY-LINE WALK-THROUGH

Line	Lawyer's Use Case	Common Manipulation	SPOT THE RED FLAG!
REVENUE	Breach-of-contract damages; earn-outs	Channel-stuffing, bill-and-hold, round-trip sales	
COST OF GOODS SOLD	Margin covenants; inventory disputes	Switching from FIFO to LIFO; overstated work-in-progress	
GROSS PROFIT	Royalty base in licence agreements	Mis-classifying direct labour	Revenue up >20 %,
SELLING, GENERAL & ADMINISTRATIVE (SG&A)	Reasonableness tests (derivative suits)	Capitalising routine maintenance	operating cash flat
OPERATING INCOME & EBIT	Solvency opinions; valuation multiples	Adjusted EBIT that omits recurring costs	investigate cut-off
INTEREST EXPENSE	Debt-service coverage tests	Capitalised interest on construction in progress	
TAX EXPENSE	Transfer-pricing, deferred-tax asset valuation	Releasing valuation allowance to boost earnings	
NET INCOME	EPS claims; dividend restrictions	One-time gains below the line; changing discontinued-operations threshold	

Figure 3.3: Line-by-line walk-through

Figure 3.3 provides a detailed view of important income statement line items, illustrating their significance in legal contexts and identifying common manipulations that can lead to disputes or regulatory scrutiny.

Each line item, ranging from revenue to net income, serves as a critical data point for lawyers addressing issues such as contract breaches, financial covenant compliance, valuation disputes, and allegations of mismanagement or fraud.

Stakeholders can better navigate the intersection of financial reporting and legal accountability if they fully understand these line items, their legal applications, and how they can be manipulated.

- **Revenue or Fees Earned**: This line represents the top line of the income statement, reflecting income earned from goods sold or services rendered. Lawyers frequently rely on revenue figures to calculate damages in breach-of-contract cases (e.g., lost sales due to a supplier's failure to deliver) or to determine payouts in earn-out agreements tied to revenue targets in mergers and acquisitions. However, revenue is susceptible to manipulation through practices such as channel stuffing (overloading distributors with excess inventory), bill-and-hold schemes (recording sales for goods not yet delivered), and round-trip sales (fictitious transactions designed to inflate revenue), all of which can mislead stakeholders and trigger legal disputes.

- **Cost of Goods Sold (COGS) or Cost of Services**: The COGS represents the direct costs incurred in producing goods or delivering services, including materials and labor. Lawyers analyze COGS in the context of margin covenants in loan agreements, which often require a minimum gross margin, as well as in inventory disputes, such as those arising in partnership dissolutions or bankruptcy proceedings. Manipulations here include switching inventory valuation methods from FIFO (First-In, First-Out) to LIFO (Last-In, First-Out) to alter Cost of Goods Sold (COGS) in times of rising prices. While this is a legitimate accounting choice, it can be used deceptively to manipulate margins or to overstate work-in-progress inventory, which reduces COGS and inflates profits.

- **Gross Profit**: Calculated as Revenue minus Cost of Goods Sold (COGS), gross profit measures the profitability of core operations before accounting for overhead costs. In legal contexts, it often serves as the royalty base in licensing agreements, where royalties are calculated as a percentage of gross profit from licensed products or services. A common manipulation is misclassifying direct labor (which should be included in Cost of Goods Sold, or COGS) as an operating expense, thereby inflating gross profit and potentially increasing royalty payouts or misleading stakeholders about profitability.

Gross Profit → Solvency

If gross profit is consistently negative, the company may struggle to generate sufficient cash to cover other expenses, such as debt payments, which could signal potential financial distress or insolvency.

Lawyer's Tip

Solvency analysis for lawyers: Essential calculations:

- Track gross profit margin trends over 3+ years
- Compare to industry benchmarks (RMA Annual Statement Studies)
- Request monthly gross margin reports from management
- Calculate gross margin per business segment/product line

Insolvency red flag: Negative gross profit for 2+ consecutive quarters

---

Lawyer Application

Gross Profit in Bankruptcy:

- A declining gross margin across quarters can justify creditors' push for liquidation.

- In fraud cases, inflated gross profit often indicates premature or fictitious revenue.

- Always request segment gross margins in due diligence; loss leaders generally hide here.

- **Selling, General, and Administrative (SG&A):** SG&A encompasses overhead costs, including marketing, executive salaries, and office expenses. In shareholders' derivative suits, lawyers usually analyze SG&A for reasonableness, since excessive executive spending may indicate mismanagement or breach of fiduciary duty. A common manipulation involves improperly capitalizing routine maintenance costs, such as recording equipment repairs as long-term assets instead of expensing them immediately. Doing this reduces SG&A in the current period and inflates operating income, potentially masking inefficiencies or misleading shareholders.

- **Operating Income and EBIT:** Operating income reflects profit from core business activities after SG&A, while EBIT (Earnings Before Interest and Taxes) may include non-operating items like investment income. For simplicity, they are often used interchangeably in valuation, though the distinction matters in precise accounting. A common manipulation is presenting an "Adjusted EBIT" that excludes recurring costs (e.g., regular litigation expenses), overstating profitability, and misleading stakeholders in solvency or valuation analyses.

Operating Income & EBIT → Valuation

EBIT focuses on the company's overall earning power, excluding variables related to financing and taxation that may differ between companies or jurisdictions. It is used in valuations employing multiples, such as applying an (x) EBIT multiple in mergers and acquisitions

(M&A) deals, and to estimate damages (loss of profit) from breaches.

Lawyer's Tip

Valuation dispute ammunition: Critical discovery items:

- Management projections vs. actual performance
- Comparable company analysis from investment bankers
- Board valuation committee meeting minutes
- "Management adjustments" to EBITDA calculations

Damages multiplier: Use industry-standard EBIT multiples from recent transactions

---

Lawyer Application

- Courts may accept adjusted EBIT as a damage proxy, provided that the underlying assumptions are defensible.

- Hidden discretionary expenses (such as excess marketing and personal travel) can distort the results.

- Collaborate with forensic accountants to sanitize EBIT inputs.

- **Interest Expense:** This line captures the cost of borrowed funds. Lawyers examine interest expense in debt-service coverage tests, a covenant metric that ensures a company can cover interest payments with its operating earnings (i.e., EBIT / Interest Expense). Companies may manipulate this by over-capitalizing interest on construction projects, reducing reported interest expense, and improving coverage ratios, which can obscure financial strain and lead to disputes with lenders.

- **Tax Expense:** Tax expense reflects the company's tax liability for the period. Lawyers analyze it in transfer-pricing disputes, ensuring that intercompany transactions comply with tax laws, and in deferred-tax asset (DTA) valuation, where DTAs from tax losses are assessed for recoverability. A common manipulation is releasing a valuation allowance on DTAs, claiming they are now realizable, which reduces tax expense and boosts net income, often used to artificially inflate earnings during a turnaround period.

- **Net Income:** Net income, the bottom line of the income statement, represents the business's total profit after all expenses, including operating costs, interest, and taxes. Earnings management or manipulations typically involve reclassifying items to influence how net income is perceived. For example, firms may emphasize one-time gains as non-recurring, while still allowing them to boost net income, or shift significant losses into the discontinued operations section, making ongoing earnings appear stronger. Both tactics inflate reported performance.

Net Income → Covenant Compliance

Net Income is generally used in covenants because it reflects an entity's overall profitability and ability to repay debt.

Lawyer's Tip

- Covenant litigation tactics: Must-have evidence:
- Original loan agreement and all amendments
- Compliance certificates filed with lender
- Internal emails discussing covenant calculations
- Accountant work papers for covenant computations

Plaintiff strategy: Challenge one-time adjustments and calculation methodologies

Defense strategy: Establish consistent application of covenant definitions and industry-standard

Lawyer Application

- If a company's net income falls below the covenant threshold, it may default on its loan, allowing lenders to demand immediate repayment or take legal action, or trigger dividend restrictions.
- In disputes over covenant breaches, lawyers may argue whether net income was calculated correctly (e.g., whether one-time expenses were properly accounted for).
Example: A loan covenant requires the company to maintain a minimum annual net income of $500,000. If net income drops to $400,000 due to a one-time expense, the lender might claim a breach. The company's lawyer could argue the covenant should exclude one-time items, avoiding default.

Depreciation & Amortization (D&A)

Depreciation (for tangible assets, such as equipment or buildings) and amortization (for intangible assets, such as patents or software) are systematic allocations of cost over time. They reduce reported net income but do not represent actual cash outflows during the period.

- **Why companies use them**: To spread out the expense of an asset over its useful life.

- **How they appear**: As non-cash operating expenses, often grouped in Selling, General, and Administrative (SG&A) costs.

Lawyer Application

- Many deals and disputes rely on EBITDA (Earnings Before Interest, Taxes, Depreciation, and Amortization) as a performance or valuation metric. While EBITDA strips out D&A to approximate cash flow, it can overstate financial health by ignoring the real need to reinvest in assets.

- Manipulation risk: Companies may extend the "useful life" of assets, lowering depreciation expense and inflating earnings.

- Always ask yourself: Does excluding D&A distort the accurate financial picture?

5 Income Statement Diagnostic Drill

When reviewing any income statement, ask these questions in order:

 The Lawyer's Income Statement Diagnostic

Step 1:
→ **Revenue:** Does growth match industry trends? Any unusual spikes?

Step 2:
→ **COGS:** Are margins consistent year-over-year?

Step 3:
→ **Operating Expenses:** Any items that should be capitalized or vice versa?

Step 4:
→ **Non-Operating:** What's hiding in "Other Income"?

Step 5:
→ **Tax Rate:** Unusually low? Check for deferred tax manipulation

Figure 3.4: The Lawyer's Income Statement Diagnostic

6 Income Statement Margins & Coverage Ratios

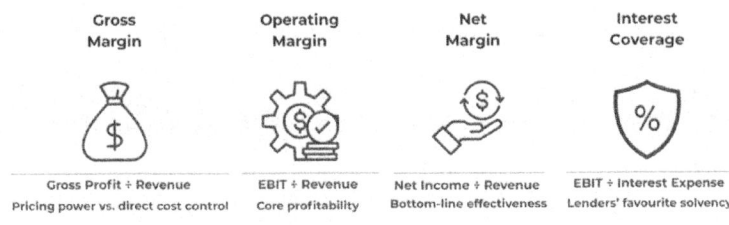

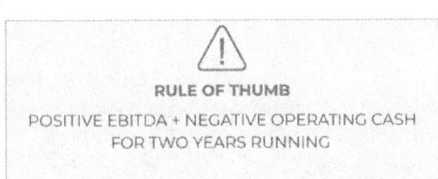

Figure 3.5: Income Statement Margins and Coverage Ratios

Figure 3.5 outlines four key financial metrics: Gross Margin, Operating Margin, Net Margin, and Interest-Coverage Ratio. They are essential for evaluating a company's profitability, efficiency, and financial stability.

These ratios convert income statement data into standardized percentages or multiples, offering quick insights into a company's operational performance and its ability to meet obligations.

For business leaders, investors, and lawyers, these metrics are key tools in assessing pricing strategies, cost management, overall profitability, and solvency, often playing a pivotal role in legal disputes, financial negotiations, and regulatory compliance.

Lawyer's Tip

Ratio manipulation detection: Warning signs to investigate:

- Sudden improvement in ratios near covenant test dates
- Ratios that improve while absolute numbers decline
- "Pro forma" ratio calculations excluding normal items
- Ratios calculated differently than industry standard

Discovery gold mine: Monthly ratio calculations vs. quarterly reported ratios

---

- **Gross Margin** = Gross Profit ÷ Revenue

This ratio measures the percentage of revenue remaining after deducting the Cost of Goods Sold (COGS), which, as mentioned earlier, includes direct costs such as materials and labor. A higher gross margin indicates strong pricing power, or effective control over direct costs.

For example, in the case of Coca-Cola, with a gross margin of 61% it retains $0.61 of every revenue dollar after covering direct costs.

In legal contexts, gross margin is usually scrutinized in disputes over pricing strategies or cost allocation, or in bankruptcy proceedings to assess whether a company can cover its core costs and remain viable.

- Operating Margin = EBIT ÷ Revenue

The Operating Margin reflects the percentage of revenue that remains after deducting all operating expenses (including Cost of Goods Sold and Selling, General, and Administrative expenses) but before deducting interest and taxes, often approximated as EBIT (Earnings Before Interest and Taxes). It measures core profitability, focusing on the efficiency of a company's primary business activities.

A higher operating margin suggests better operational management and profitability. For instance, in the case of Coca-Cola, an operating margin of 31% means $0.31 of every revenue dollar is profit from core operations.

Lawyers typically use this metric in valuation disputes, such as determining a fair business value in M&A litigation or in solvency opinions, as it indicates whether the company's operations generate sufficient profit to sustain itself, a key consideration in restructuring or bankruptcy cases.

- **Net Margin** = Net Income ÷ Revenue

This ratio represents the percentage of revenue that translates into net income, the final profit after all expenses, including operating costs, interest, taxes, and one-time items. Net margin is a measure of a company's bottom-line effectiveness, indicating the percentage of profit it ultimately retains.

A net margin of 23% means $0.23 of every revenue dollar Coca-Cola gets becomes profit available to shareholders.

In legal settings, net margin is key for assessing compliance with financial covenants that restrict dividends based on net income levels, as well as in securities litigation where shareholders may claim that earnings (and thus net margins) were misstated, potentially impacting stock prices or investor decisions.

- **Interest-Coverage** = EBIT ÷ Interest Expense

The Interest-Coverage ratio measures a company's ability to pay interest on its debt, and it is calculated by dividing EBIT by interest expense.

Coca-Cola's ratio of 8.9, for example, indicates the company generates nine times more EBIT than needed to cover interest payments.

This metric is typically used by lenders because it gauges a company's solvency, specifically, its ability to service its debt without defaulting.

In legal contexts, interest coverage is central to debt-related disputes, such as when a lender claims a covenant breach due to a low ratio, or in bankruptcy proceedings where lawyers argue whether a company's solvency justifies restructuring rather than liquidation.

Excerpt from Credit Agreement

(j) The Borrower must, starting on December 31, 2014, comply with the following financial ratios, calculated once a year by the Lender on the basis of the Borrower's annual Financial Statements delivered pursuant to item "(a)" above:

(i) Current Ratio equal to or greater than 1.3;
(ii) Debt-to-Equity Ratio equal to or less than 1.5; and
(iii) EBIT / Interest Expense equal to or grearter than 2.0 for 2014-15 and 2.5 for subsequent years.

Figure 3.6: Excerpt from Credit Agreement

These ratios are more than financial indicators; they are vital tools for decision-making and legal analysis.

Lawyers can better comprehend the relationship between financial performance and legal accountability, thereby ensuring transparency and fairness in business dealings, if they grasp these metrics.

Quick Reference

Gross Margin (Gross Profit ÷ Revenue): Pricing power

Operating Margin (EBIT ÷ Revenue): Management efficiency

Net Margin (Net Income ÷ Revenue): Bottom-line effectiveness

Interest Coverage (EBIT ÷ Interest): Debt-paying ability

Figure 3.7: Quick Reference: Income Statement Ratios

A company with declining margins may face challenges in pricing, cost control, or overall profitability, which could lead to disputes with stakeholders or breaches of loan agreements. Similarly, a low interest-coverage ratio can signal financial distress, prompting creditors to take legal action.

Lawyer's Tip

- Ratio manipulation detection: Key documents to subpoena:
- Monthly ratio calculations vs. quarterly reported ratios
- Board committee discussions of covenant tests
- Management emails near quarter-end
- Ratios calculated differently than industry standard

Red flag threshold: Any ratio improving >20% quarter-over-quarter

Lawyer's Rule of Thumb

Any margin declining for two consecutive years warrants investigation...

Figure 3.8: Lawyer's Rule of Thumb. Declining Margin

7 Quarter-End Profit and Loss Statement ("P&L") for ABC Law LLP

Let's return to **ABC Law LLP**, our litigation boutique introduced in chapter 1. We'll walk through a quarter-end income statement to show you exactly how the numbers connect and where the legal landmines hide. Pay special attention to how a single misclassification can compromise loan covenants and trigger legal nightmares.

INCOME STATEMENT

Item	Amount (US$ '000)	
Professional Fees Earned	680	
Total Revenue		680
Associate & Staff Wages	(340)	
Matter-Specific Outsourcing	(55)	
Gross Profit		285
Rent & Utilities	(80)	
Marketing, Admin, G&A	(60)	
Operating Income (EBIT)		145
Partner Draws (treated in equity, not expense)	---	
Interest on Credit Line	(15)	
Income Tax (@24 %)	(31)	
Net Income		99

Figure 3.9: Income Statement

Figure 3.9 presents a simplified quarter-end P&L statement for ABC Law LLP, with amounts in thousands of U.S. dollars, and demonstrates how a professional services firm applies accounting principles to construct its income statement, while highlighting a critical legal and financial consideration regarding the classification of partner draws.

By walking through each line item, we can see how revenue, expenses, and profit are calculated, and why accurate classification is fundamental to avoiding misstating financial performance and breaching legal obligations such as loan covenants. We suggest reading or refreshing our accrual accounting comments in the Accounting Assumptions, Principles, and Constraints before moving forward.

- **Professional Fees Earned**: This represents the core revenue ABC Law LLP earns from legal services provided to clients during the quarter, totaling $680,000. These fees are recognized when the services are performed, adhering to the accrual principle, regardless of when clients pay (e.g., a brief drafted in October is recorded as revenue even if payment arrives in December).

- **Total Revenue**: The sum of professional fees earned and reimbursable client costs, totaling $680,000, reflects the firm's overall revenue for the quarter.

- **Associate & Staff Wages**: This expense ($340,000) includes salaries paid to associates and support staff directly involved in delivering legal services. As a direct cost, it is subtracted from revenue to calculate gross profit, following the matching principle, which ensures costs are recorded in the same period as the revenue they help generate.

- **Matter-Specific Outsourcing**: This ($55,000) expense covers the costs of outsourcing specific legal tasks, such as hiring external researchers or consultants. Like wages, it's a direct cost tied to revenue-generating activities and is deducted to compute gross profit.

- **Gross Profit**: Calculated as Total Revenue $680,000 minus Associate & Staff Wages ($340,000) and Matter-Specific Outsourcing ($55,000), gross profit amounts to $285,000. This metric shows the firm's profitability after covering direct costs, providing key information about its ability to manage the cost of delivering services.

- **Rent & Utilities**: This ($80,000) expense covers overhead costs for office space and utilities, which are not directly tied to specific matters but are necessary for operational purposes. These are classified as operating expenses.

- **Marketing, Admin, G&A**: General and administrative (G&A) expenses, totaling ($60,000), cover costs like marketing, office supplies, and administrative salaries. These overhead costs are also subtracted as operating expenses.

- **Operating Income or EBIT**: Gross Profit of $285,000 minus Rent & Utilities ($80,000) and Marketing, Admin, G&A

($60,000) yields an operating income of $145,000. As mentioned before, often approximated as EBIT (Earnings Before Interest and Taxes), this figure represents the firm's profitability from core operations, excluding financing costs and taxes. It's a key metric for assessing how efficient operations are and is used in loan covenants or valuation analyses.

- **Partner Draws (treated in equity, not expense)**: Partner draws, the amounts partners withdraw as compensation, are not listed as an expense on the P&L. Instead, they are treated as distributions of equity, deducted after net income is calculated. Misclassifying them as a salary expense would reduce operating income and net income, potentially violating financial covenants tied to profitability metrics, such as EBIT.

For example, a $100,000 partner draw misclassified as salary would lower EBIT from $145,000 to $45,000, potentially breaching a loan covenant requiring a minimum EBIT of $100,000. This misclassification could result in disputes with lenders, who rely on accurate EBIT figures to assess solvency, or with partners, if profit distributions are understated. Proper classification ensures financial transparency and compliance with legal and contractual obligations.

Lawyer's Tip

Law firm financial analysis: Key issues for law firm disputes:

- Partner compensation vs. salary classification affects EBITDA
- Work-in-progress valuation can manipulate current assets
- Client cost advances impact working capital calculations
- Unbilled time recognition varies between firms

Always verify partner draw treatment before covenant calculations

---

- **Interest on Credit Line**: This ($15,000) expense represents interest paid on a credit line used to finance operations, reflecting the cost of borrowed funds. It's deducted after operating income, as it relates to financing rather than core operations.

- **Income Tax @24%:** Income tax expense, calculated at a 24% rate on taxable income [Operating Income of $145,000 minus Interest of $15,000 = $130,000], amounts to $31,200 [$130,000 × 24%]. This is an estimate for illustration purposes, as actual tax calculations may require additional adjustments.

- **Net Income**: The final profit, or net income, is $99,000, calculated as Operating Income of $145,000 minus Interest ($15,000) and Income Tax ($31,000). This bottom-line figure represents the profit available to the firm after all expenses, which can be distributed to partners or retained for future use.

Each line item demonstrated a deliberate application of accounting principles, such as accrual and matching, while the takeaway highlights the legal consequences of misclassification. For law firms and similar entities, it is key to understand and apply these principles to maintain trust with stakeholders and avoid costly disputes.

The ABC Law LLP example demonstrates that proper classification safeguards you from covenant breaches, but what about when companies intentionally manipulate their financial numbers? Every top corporate lawyer or litigator should have a mental checklist of red flags that signal potential fraud or misrepresentation. Here's yours: Five warning signs that should make you dig deeper immediately.

8 Income Statement Red-Flag Checklist for Lawyers

Red flags in income statements are often buried beneath plausible explanations. But if you're a lawyer working on a deal, a shareholder dispute, or a covenant breach, your job is to ask the uncomfortable questions before your client becomes the next headline.

The 60-Second Fraud Detector

⚑	**Revenue vs. Cash Flow:**	Revenue up 30%, cash flow flat? Investigate
⚑	**"Other Income" Size:**	> 10% of operating income? Dig deeper
⚑	**Inventory Method Changes:**	Timing Matters - Why Change Now?
⚑	**EBITDA vs. EBIT Gap:**	Huge gap = potential expense capitalization
⚑	**"Non-Recurring" Items:**	If it happens every year, it's recurring

Figure 3.10: The 60-Second Fraud Detector. Income Statement

Revenue Growth ≫ Operating-Cash Growth: This red flag occurs when revenue growth significantly outpaces the growth in operating cash flow (as reported on the cash-flow statement – which we will review in the next chapter).

Under the accrual principle, revenue is recorded when earned, not when cash is received, which can lead to discrepancies.

For example, if a company reports 30% revenue growth but operating cash flow grows only 5%, it may be recognizing revenue prematurely through practices such as channel stuffing or bill-and-hold schemes, without collecting the corresponding cash. This can inflate reported earnings, misleading stakeholders and result in lawsuits from investors or disputes in earn-out agreements where revenue targets are a factor.

Lawyers should investigate whether the revenue recognition aligns with accounting standards to ensure it accurately reflects genuine economic activity.

Lawyer's Tip

Revenue Recognition Red Flags:

- December invoices for January services
- Revenue up 30%, cash flow flat
- Unusual Q4 spikes near covenant tests

Look for these documents: Sales contracts, shipping records, customer correspondence

---

Large "Other Income" Hiding Restructuring Charges: "Other Income" on the income statement includes non-operating items, such as gains from asset sales or investment income.

A large or inconsistent "Other Income" figure may conceal restructuring charges, like severance costs or write-downs from closing a business unit, by netting them against unrelated gains. This obscures the true financial impact of restructuring, making the company appear more profitable than it is.

For instance, a $1 million gain from selling an asset might offset a $1 million restructuring charge, resulting in a net "Other Income" of $0, hiding the operational strain. Lawyers should scrutinize this line item in valuation disputes or solvency opinions, as it can mislead stakeholders about the company's core profitability and sustainability, potentially violating fiduciary obligations or triggering regulatory procedures.

Lawyer's Tip

Piercing the "Other Income" veil: Essential discovery requests:

- Detailed general ledger for "Other Income" accounts
- Asset sale agreements and appraisals
- Restructuring committee meeting minutes
- CFO/Controller emails mentioning "netting" or "offsetting"

Investigation focus: Any "Other Income" >5% of operating income

---

Swing from FIFO to Average-Cost Inventory in Inflationary Year: This red flag involves a change in inventory valuation method from FIFO (First-In, First-Out) to Average-Cost during a period of rising prices.

Under the FIFO method, older (cheaper) inventory is expensed first, resulting in a lower Cost of Goods Sold (COGS) and higher reported profits in an inflationary environment. Switching to Average-Cost, which smooths out costs by averaging, increases COGS (as it includes more recent, higher-priced inventory), reducing gross profit and net income.

While this change is a legitimate accounting choice under accounting standards, making the switch in an inflationary year may be a deliberate attempt to lower taxable income.

Lawyers should investigate the intent behind the change, especially in disputes involving inventory valuation or tax compliance, as it could signal an attempt to obscure the company's true financial position.

> **Lawyer's Tip**
>
> Inventory method change analysis: Critical evidence to obtain:
>
> - Board resolutions authorizing accounting changes
> - External auditor management letters and recommendations
> - Monthly gross margin trending reports
> - Tax advisor correspondence about inventory methods
>
> Timing red flag: Changes made in Q4 or during covenant stress

EBITDA Positive, EBIT Negative (Look for Capitalizing Expenses): This warning sign arises when EBITDA (Earnings Before Interest, Taxes, Depreciation, and Amortization) is positive, but EBIT (Earnings Before Interest and Taxes) is negative.

Since EBITDA excludes depreciation and amortization, a significant gap between the two metrics typically indicates high depreciation/amortization expenses, which may result from capitalizing expenses that should have been expensed. For example, capitalizing routine maintenance costs (instead of recording them as SG&A expenses) creates an asset that is depreciated over time, reducing EBIT but not EBITDA. This can inflate perceived profitability, misleading stakeholders in solvency opinions or valuation analyses.

Lawyers should examine whether the company is violating the matching principle by capitalizing normal operating expenses, as this could lead to shareholder lawsuits for misrepresentation or breaches of loan covenants tied to EBIT thresholds.

Lawyer's Tip

Expense capitalization detection: Target documents for review:

- Capital expenditure approval workflows
- Asset capitalization policies and changes
- Detailed depreciation schedules by asset category
- Internal audit reports on capitalization practices

Mathematical clue: EBITDA-EBIT gap >15% of revenue warrants investigation

---

Repeated "Non-Recurring" Charges That Recur Every Year: Companies may classify certain expenses, like litigation settlements or restructuring costs, as "non-recurring" to suggest they are one-time events, encouraging stakeholders to focus on adjusted earnings metrics (e.g., "Adjusted EBIT"). However, if these charges recur annually, they are effectively recurring operational costs that should be included in core profitability calculations.

For instance, a company reporting $500,000 in "non-recurring" litigation charges every year for five consecutive years is likely facing systemic legal issues, rather than isolated events. This misclassification can overstate profitability, misleading investors or lenders in valuation disputes or assessments of covenant compliance.

Lawyers should challenge the "non-recurring" label in securities litigation or due diligence, ensuring that these costs are appropriately reflected in financial statements to avoid allegations of fraud or breaches of fiduciary duty.

Lawyer's Tip

Challenging "non-recurring" labels: Powerful discovery tools:

- 3-5 years of earnings call transcripts
- Investor presentation slides excluding these items
- Management bonus calculations and adjustments
- Credit agreement covenant calculation worksheets

Smoking gun: Same expense type labeled "non-recurring" 2+ years

---

This checklist serves as a practical tool for lawyers navigating the complexities of financial statements. Each red flag relates back to fundamental accounting principles.

By identifying these issues early, lawyers can protect their clients from financial misrepresentations, ensure compliance with contractual and regulatory obligations, and strengthen their cases in disputes involving damages, valuation, or solvency.

Investigation Triggers

- Any ratio changing >25% year-over-year
- Footnotes longer than the financial statements
- "Pro forma" numbers that exclude "one-time" items

Figure 3.11: Investigation Triggers. Income Statement

9 Stories from the Trenches: When Income Statements Lie

These red flags might seem academic until you see their real-world consequences. The following war stories come from actual cases where lawyers who spotted these warning signs saved their clients millions, and where lawyers who missed them paid dearly. Each story illustrates why financial literacy is not only helpful for lawyers but indispensable for their success.

The Phantom-Invoice Bonus: A tech CEO backdated $2M in software licenses to hit revenue targets and unlock bonuses. Discovery revealed the "licenses" were never delivered. Result: Bonus clawback, and $10M in damages under anti-fraud statutes.

Fixed-Fee Litigation Trap: A law firm booked $500K in fees when signing a fixed-fee litigation contract. When they lost the case, they had to refund everything but had already distributed "profits" to partners. Prior-year statements required restatement.

The Unicorn's Adjusted Reality: A startup's "Adjusted EBITDA" excluded stock compensation and "customer acquisition costs", essentially all their expenses. The buyer discovered this during due diligence and cut the acquisition price in half.

Stadium-Sale Mirage: A sports franchise showed a net profit, but operating losses surfaced once a one-off land gain was stripped out, according to a court-adjusted valuation in a divorce proceeding.

Lawyer's Tip

Learning from others' mistakes: Litigation prevention checklist:

- Always verify revenue recognition policies during due diligence
- Request "management adjustments" explanations in writing
- Compare preliminary vs. final financial statements
- Document timing of any accounting policy changes

Settlement leverage: Real-world precedents show damages can exceed multiple times the misstatement

---

10 Cash Flow Connection

These stories all share a common thread: The income statement told one story, but the cash-flow statement said another. Understanding this disconnect is perhaps the most powerful tool in a lawyer's financial arsenal. When profit and cash don't match, someone's usually lying, and the cash-flow statement will tell you who.

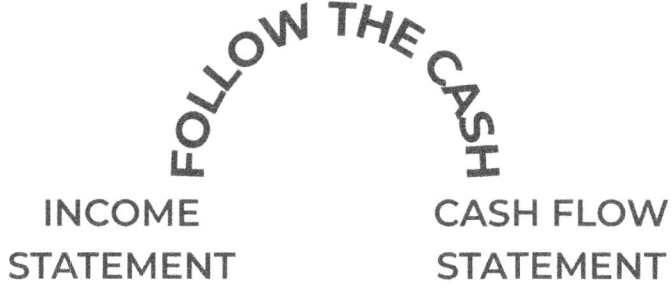

FOLLOW THE CASH

INCOME STATEMENT

Item	Amount ($ '000)
Professional Fees Earned	680
Total Revenue	680
Associate & Staff Wages	(340)
Matter-Specific Outsourcing	(55)
Gross Profit	285
Rent & Utilities	(80)
Marketing, Admin, G&A	(60)
Operating Income (EBIT)	145
Partner Draws (treated in equity, not expense)	---
Interest on Credit Line	(15)
Income Tax (@24 %)	(31)
Net Income	99

CASH FLOW STATEMENT

Item	Amount ($ '000)
Net Income	99
+ Non-Cash Adjustments	xxx
+ Changes in Working Capital	xxx
= Net Cash from Operations	xxx

Figure 3.12: Income Statement and Cash Flow Connection

Where Profit Goes to Hide

Net income is just the starting point for operating cash flow. The magic happens in the adjustments:

The Formula: Net Income + Depreciation ± Working Capital Changes = Operating Cash Flow

It is crucial to comprehend the relationship between net income and operating cash flow, a fundamental concept for assessing a company's financial health. Net income is only the first line of *operating cash flow*. Add back non-cash charges (depreciation, amortization), subtract increases in receivables, and add decreases in payables.

Operating cash flow, reported in the cash-flow statement, measures the cash generated from a company's core operations, providing a clearer picture of liquidity than net income alone. Since net income is based on accrual accounting, it includes non-cash items and timing differences that must be adjusted to reflect actual cash movements.

The Danger signal: Three years of positive net income +

negative operating cash.

What This Means:

- Customers aren't paying (receivables growing).

- Inventory is building up (cash tied up in stock).

- Revenue recognition is getting aggressive.

The danger signal described serves as a warning for lawyers and financial analysts, indicating potential manipulations that could end in disputes or regulatory reviews.

In the Cash Flow chapter, we explain how to build a cash-flow statement starting with net income, the bottom line of the income statement.

Now you have the tools to read an income statement like a financial detective, spot the red flags like a seasoned corporate attorney or litigator, and connect the dots like an expert witness. But knowledge without practice is just theory. The exercises at the end of the chapter will help you apply everything you've learned to real scenarios you'll

face in practice

Lawyer's Tip

Cash vs. profit investigation: Critical analysis steps:

- Reconcile quarterly net income to operating cash flow
- Track accounts receivable aging and write-offs
- Analyze inventory turnover trends
- Request monthly cash flow projections vs. actual

Fraud indicator: 3+ years of positive income but negative operating cash flow

---

Key Takeaways

Key Takeaways

- The income statement tells a story of performance over time, not a static picture.
- Revenue and expense recognition rules create judgment calls; lawyers probe those calls.
- Manipulations are common at quarter-end, especially around revenue recognition.
- Margins and ratios convert data into solvency and profitability tests.
- For lawyers, dissecting line items reveals fraud, breaches of covenants, and mismanagement.

Callback

Those two New Year's Eve invoices? A five-minute cut-off test: "Were goods delivered, or services rendered by December 31?" - would have exposed them.

In the **Accounting Principles chapter**, we saw how revenue recognition and matching support reporting rules. In this chapter, we saw those principles applied and how they are sometimes bent in practice.

Segue

To uncover whether reported profits translate into cash, we now turn to the **cash-flow statement**.

11 Exercises

Lawyer's Tip

Practice makes perfect: Real-world application:

- Use these exercises with actual client financial statements
- Create template document request lists based on red flags found
- Practice explaining financial concepts using simple language
- Build expert witness examination outlines around these concepts

Career advantage: Financial literacy sets lawyers apart from the competition

11.1 Revenue Recognition Check

A company with a fiscal year ending December 31, 2024, issues five invoices in December. Based on the accrual principle, determine which invoices belong in 2024's revenue.

a. Invoice 1: Issued Dec 1, 2024, for consulting services completed Nov 30, 2024, $5,000.

b. Invoice 2: Issued Dec 10, 2024, for legal services to be completed Jan 15, 2025, $3,000.

c. Invoice 3: Issued Dec 15, 2024, for a product delivered Dec

20, 2024, $8,000.

   d. Invoice 4: Issued Dec 20, 2024, for a subscription starting Jan 1, 2025, $2,000.

   e. Invoice 5: Issued Dec 31, 2024, for services completed Dec 31, 2024, $4,000.

Follow-up: If Invoice 3 was recorded in the wrong fiscal year, how might this impact a breach-of-contract damages calculation?

11.2 Covenant Breach

A loan covenant requires a minimum annual net income of $500,000. The company reports $400,000, citing one-time restructuring costs. How would you argue this case?

11.3 Margin Analysis

Gross margin has fallen from 40% to 25% in one year, while revenue grew. What legal implications could this have in a bankruptcy proceeding?

5 THE CASH-FLOW STATEMENT — FOLLOWING THE MONEY WHEN PROFIT ISN'T CASH

A biotech client had just closed a $2.1M venture round. Their income statement looked healthy, and projections promised profitability within a year.

But on Thursday afternoon, the CFO called: They couldn't make Friday's payroll. It turns out that the revenue had been booked, the margins looked fine, but the cash never arrived. Delayed receivables, overestimated billing speed, and overambitious headcount expansion had drained the account.

The income statement told a story. The cash-flow statement said the truth.

While revenue recognition offers room for creative interpretation and balance sheets can hide problems in footnotes, **cash flow cuts through the accounting fiction**.

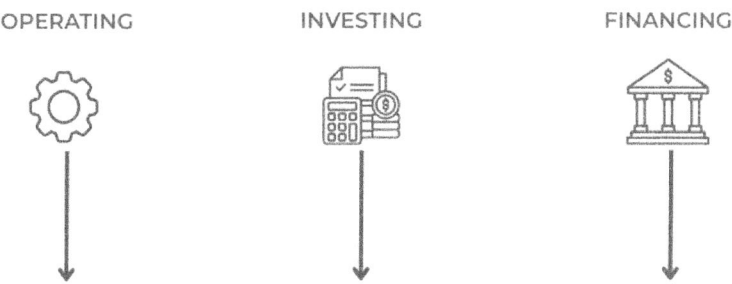

Figure 4.1: Cash-Flow Funnel

Chapter Thesis

The cash-flow statement converts accrual accounting back into the universal language of money. It reveals where cash is truly generated or consumed, often exposing truths that the income statement and balance sheet conceal. For lawyers, it is the frontline test of solvency, covenant compliance, and fraudulent transfers.

📷 Chapter Snapshot – Cash-flow Statement

Chapter Essentials

- **Purpose:** Tracks liquidity across operating, investing, and financing activities.

- **Contrast:** Profit ≠ Cash: Companies can be profitable yet insolvent.

- **Legal relevance:** Crucial for solvency tests, damages, covenant disputes, and fraud cases.

- **Red flag:** Positive net income with negative operating cash flow is generally a danger signal.

1 The Cash Flow Statement

This chapter introduces the cash-flow statement, a critical component of a company's financial reporting, and explains its role in relation to the income statement and the balance sheet.

Together, these three financial statements provide a comprehensive view of a company's financial health: The balance sheet shows *position* (assets, liabilities, and equity at a specific point in time), the income statement measures *performance* (profitability over a period, *on an accrual basis*), and the cash-flow statement reveals *liquidity* - how cash moves between two balance-sheet snapshots (i.e., from the beginning to the end of the period).

Cash Flow Statement

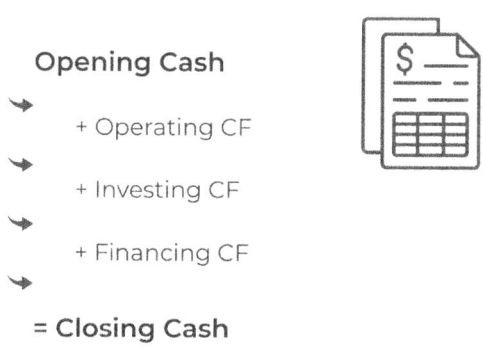

Opening Cash
→ + Operating CF
→ + Investing CF
→ + Financing CF
= Closing Cash

Figure 4.2: Cash Flow Statement

If a profitable company is bleeding cash, the evidence is here first.

Cash, for cash-flow statement purposes, refers to cash and cash equivalents. Cash includes currency, checks deposited or not, and bank deposits that can be withdrawn without prior notice, condition, or penalty. Cash equivalents mean investments that can convert to cash quickly and that have maturity dates no longer than 90 days.

The cash-flow statement is structured to show the net change in a company's cash balance over a period, breaking down cash movements into three categories:

Opening Cash: This represents the cash balance at the beginning of the period, as reported on the balance sheet at the start of the period. It serves as the starting point for tracking cash flows.

Operating Cash Flow (OCF): This section reflects cash generated or used by the company's core business activities, such as selling goods or providing services, cash received from customers (collections), and cash paid to suppliers or employees (payments).

It begins with net income (from the income statement) and adjusts for non-cash items (e.g., depreciation) and changes in working capital (e.g., accounts receivable and accounts payable).

Positive operating cash flow indicates that a company can sustain its operations using cash generated from its primary activities, whereas negative operating cash flow may signal liquidity issues.
From a lawyer's perspective, operating cash flow is the first test of solvency: If a company cannot generate positive cash flow from its core business, it may struggle to meet its obligations, signaling potential insolvency - a key concern in bankruptcy proceedings.

It's also critical for covenant compliance, as loan agreements usually require a minimum operating cash flow to ensure the borrower can service debt. Additionally, in litigation, operating cash flow is used to calculate damages for lost profits (e.g., in a breach-of-contract case), as it reflects the cash a company would have generated had the breach not occurred.

For example, if a company loses a client due to a supplier's failure, the lost operating cash flow from that client's fees could quantify damages.

Investing Cash Flow (ICF): This section captures cash flows related to the acquisition or disposal of long-term assets, such as the purchase of equipment or the sale of property (capital expenditures, or capex), acquiring businesses, or selling assets or securities.

A negative cash flow often indicates an investment in growth, while a positive cash flow may reflect asset sales, which might signal financial distress if done to raise cash.

From a lawyer's lens, this section could reveal asset sales that prop up dividends. If a company sells assets to generate cash for dividend payments, it may be masking operational weaknesses, a concern in shareholder lawsuits alleging mismanagement.

It may also highlight capital expenditure cuts that defer maintenance liabilities, reducing capital expenditures (e.g., delaying equipment repairs). These cuts can inflate short-term cash flow but create future liabilities if neglected maintenance leads to breakdowns or safety issues, potentially breaching fiduciary duties or regulatory standards.

Case in point: Boeing

Boeing steadily cut back its capital expenditures as a share of sales after the early 2010s. In 2013–2014, Boeing's capex stayed around 2.4% of revenue, but from 2015 through 2018, it declined below 2%, reaching 1.7% by 2018. Spending briefly increased again to 2.4% in 2019 but dropped during the pandemic; 2.2% in 2020, and just 1.6% in 2021. Even after demand bounced back, Boeing remained cautious: 1.8% in 2022 and 1.9% in 2023, only returning to 2.4% of sales in 2024, roughly where it was a decade earlier.

Airbus, by contrast, maintained a significantly higher level of reinvestment during the same period. From 2013 to 2018, its capex ranged from 3.6% to 5.3% of sales, roughly twice that of Boeing. Even during the COVID years, Airbus kept capex at 3.5% to 3.7% of revenue, then increased investment during the recovery: 4.2% in 2022, 4.7% in 2023, and 5.2% in 2024.

Boeing's retrenchment coincided with aggressive shareholder payouts (over **$60 billion in dividends and buybacks from 2013 to 2019)** while safety lapses increased. Two fatal 737 MAX crashes, worsened by production pressures that ignored quality control, led to a **$2.5 billion deferred prosecution agreement** with the DOJ. In **January 2024**, an **Alaska Airlines 737 MAX 9** lost a door plug mid-flight, revealing systemic quality-control failures. Regulators forced Boeing to **slow production**, and the company reported **$12.1 billion in operating cash outflows in**

2024, halting its free-cash-flow recovery plans.

Year	Boeing	Airbus
2013	2.4%	5.3%
2014	2.4%	4.2%
2015	1.9%	4.5%
2016	2.0%	4.6%
2017	1.8%	3.8%
2018	1.7%	3.6%
2019	2.4%	3.0%
2020	2.2%	3.5%
2021	1.6%	3.7%
2022	1.8%	4.2%
2023	1.9%	4.7%
2024	2.4%	5.2%

Table 4.1: Capex as % of Revenue: Boeing vs. Airbus (2013-2014)

Financing Cash Flow (FCF): This section captures cash flows related to funding the business, such as borrowing from lenders, the issuance of stock, repayment of debt (short and long-term), repurchasing equity, and paying dividends or partner draws, as we will see with ABC Law LLP in subchapter 6 ahead. A positive financing cash flow might indicate new loans or equity issuance, while a negative figure could reflect debt repayment or dividend payouts.

From a lawyer's perspective, financing activities reveal whether growth is debt-funded. Heavy borrowing to finance operations (e.g., a $1 million loan to cover operating losses) may indicate unsustainable growth, raising concerns during due diligence for mergers or acquisitions.

This section also flags dividends paid with debt in cases involving fraudulent transfers. Under laws such as the Uniform Fraudulent Transfer Act or the Uniform Voidable Transfer Act, paying dividends with borrowed funds when a company is insolvent can be deemed a fraudulent transfer, allowing creditors to recover those payments and exposing directors to potential liability.

Closing Cash: The sum of the opening cash balance and the net cash flows from operating, investing, and financing activities equals the closing cash balance, which matches the cash reported on the balance sheet at the end of the period. This reconciliation ensures the cash-flow statement ties the balance sheets together, providing a clear picture of how cash moved during the period.

A warning system

The note to Figure 4.2 at the beginning of this chapter: "If a profitable company is bleeding cash, the evidence is here first", underscores the cash-flow statement's role as an early warning system.

A company may report positive net income on its income statement (indicating profitability) but still face liquidity issues if it's not generating enough cash. This ties directly to the danger signal discussed in this chapter: A mismatch between positive net income and negative operating cash flow over multiple years can indicate problems such as aging receivables or inventory buildup, often signaling potential fraud or financial distress.

For example, suppose a company reports $500,000 in net income but has a negative operating cash flow of $200,000 due to uncollected receivables. In that case, the cash-flow statement will reveal this cash bleed, alerting stakeholders to underlying issues before they fully manifest in the income statement or balance sheet.

For lawyers, the cash-flow statement is a vital tool in legal contexts such as bankruptcy proceedings, where liquidity determines a company's ability to meet obligations, or in shareholder lawsuits, where discrepancies between profitability and cash flow might indicate misrepresentation or fraud. It's also critical in assessing compliance with loan covenants, which often require a minimum level of operating cash flow or cash reserves.

By revealing how cash flows through a company, the cash-flow statement provides a reality check on reported profits, ensuring stakeholders have a transparent view of the company's financial health and enabling early intervention to mitigate legal and financial risks.

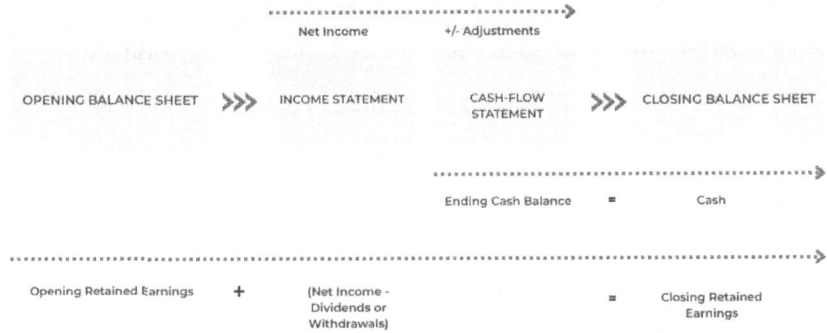

Figure 4.3: Financial-Statement Bridge

2 The Three Cash Buckets

The Three Cash Buckets

Section	What It Captures	Lawyer's Lens
Operating Activities	Day-to-day collections and payments from core business	First solvency test; covenant compliance; damages based on lost operating cash
Investing Activities	Buying and selling long-term assets, businesses, or securities	Reveals asset sales that prop up dividends; cap-ex cuts that defer maintenance - liability
Financing Activities	Borrowing, repaying, selling equity, paying dividends / draws	Shows whether growth is debt-funded; flags dividend-paid-with-debt in fraudulent-transfer cases

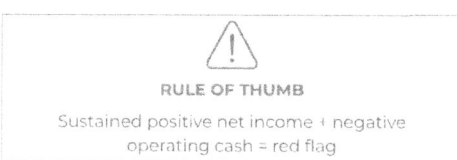

RULE OF THUMB
Sustained positive net income + negative operating cash = red flag

Figure 4.4: The Three Cash Buckets

Figure 4.4 categorizes the cash-flow statement into its three mentioned sections: Operating Activities, Investing Activities, and Financing Activities, detailing what each section captures and why it matters from a lawyer's perspective.

The accompanying rule of thumb further underscores the importance of monitoring operating cash flow in relation to net income, a recurring theme in detecting financial red flags with legal implications.

Negative operating cash flow often reveals the root cause, such as aggressive revenue recognition or hidden operational losses, prompting further investigation into the company's financial practices.

Lawyer Application

Cash from Financing in Disputes

- Check timing of loans vs. asset acquisitions: Was debt used as intended?

- Repayment mismatches or unrecorded distributions may breach debt covenants.

- Over-distribution to owners without retained earnings can violate fiduciary duties or trigger piercing-the-veil arguments.

Rule of Thumb: Sustained Positive Net Income + Negative Operating Cash = Red Flag

The three cash buckets provide a structured way to understand cash movements, but their legal significance lies in what they reveal about a company's financial reality.

Operating cash flow tests the sustainability of core operations, investing activities uncover potential asset mismanagement, and financing activities expose risky funding practices, all of which can end in disputes, from covenant breaches to fraudulent transfers.

By mastering the cash-flow statement, lawyers can identify

discrepancies between reported profits and actual liquidity, ensuring transparency and protecting stakeholders from financial misrepresentations. This section builds on earlier discussions of accrual accounting and financial red flags, equipping readers with the tools to understand the legal implications of cash flow dynamics.

Lawyer's Tip

Cash flow investigation priorities: Key documents to analyze:

- Monthly cash flow statements (not just quarterly)
- Customer payment terms and collection reports
- Vendor payment schedules and extension agreements
- Board minutes discussing cash management decisions

Red flag threshold: Operating cash flow negative for 2+ consecutive quarters

---

3 Direct vs Indirect Presentation

Direct vs Indirect Presentation

Feature	Direct Method	Indirect Method
Starts with	Cash received from customers	Net income (accrual)
Shows	Gross cash inflows / outflows	Reconciliation from profit to cash
Pros	Easy for non-accountants to read	Requires no extra ledger; quick to draft
Cons	Companies rarely track data at this detail	Obscures where cash was earned or burned

Figure 4.5: Direct vs Indirect Presentation

Regulators accept either method, but if a client offers only the indirect format, ask for a supplemental schedule of significant cash receipts and payments, as you will need it for any material transaction or in litigation.

Figure 4.5 compares the two methods for presenting the operating activities section of the cash-flow statement: The Direct Method and the Indirect Method. As introduced in this chapter, the cash-flow statement tracks the movement of cash through a company, with the operating activities section focusing on the cash generated or used by the company's core business operations.

While both methods ultimately calculate the same net operating cash flow, they differ in their approach, presentation, and utility for stakeholders, including lawyers.

Understanding these differences is key to interpreting financial statements, especially in legal contexts where cash flow data can determine business price, litigation, solvency assessments, or fraud investigations.

The recommendation to request a supplemental schedule when only the indirect method is provided underscores the practical challenges lawyers face in analyzing cash flows for legal purposes.

- Starts With

The Direct Method begins with cash received from customers, directly reporting actual cash inflows (e.g., collections from sales) and outflows (e.g., payments to suppliers or employees) related to operations.

In contrast, the Indirect Method, used predominantly, starts with net income (accrual) from the income statement and adjusts it to reflect cash flows. As discussed in earlier subchapters, net income is an accrual-based measure, meaning it includes non-cash items (e.g., depreciation) and timing differences (e.g., receivables), which must be reconciled to arrive at the operating cash flow.

- Shows

The Direct Method displays gross cash inflows and outflows, offering a breakdown of cash transactions, such as $500,000 received from customers and $300,000 paid to suppliers, resulting in a net operating cash flow. This detailed view reflects the actual cash movements in daily operations.

The Indirect Method, however, focuses on reconciling profit to cash, adjusting net income for non-cash items (e.g., adding back depreciation) and changes in working capital (e.g., subtracting increases in receivables), as outlined in subchapter 6 ahead. For example, if net income is $100,000, depreciation is $20,000, and receivables increased by $10,000, the operating cash flow would be $110,000 = $100,000 + $20,000 - $10,000.

- Pros

The Direct Method is straightforward for non-accountants to understand because it directly displays cash inflows and outflows, similar to a cash-based income statement. This clarity is beneficial for stakeholders, such as lawyers or managers, who need to grasp where cash is coming from and going without having to sift through accrual adjustments.

The Indirect Method, however, requires no extra ledger and is quick to draft, as it uses data already available from the income statement and balance sheet (e.g., net income, changes in receivables). This efficiency explains its prevalence in U.S. filings, as companies can produce it without maintaining detailed records of cash transactions.

- Cons

The Direct Method's primary drawback is that companies rarely track data at this level of detail. Most businesses use accrual accounting and don't maintain separate ledgers for cash inflows and outflows, making the Direct Method cumbersome to prepare. For example, tracking every customer payment and supplier disbursement requires additional record-keeping, which many companies avoid.

Conversely, the Indirect Method obscures where cash was earned or burned, as it focuses on adjustments rather than actual cash movements. For instance, a $50,000 increase in operating cash flow might result from reduced payables; however, the Indirect Method doesn't indicate whether this increase came from delaying supplier payments or negotiating better terms, thereby limiting its transparency.

- Accounting Standards

Both the Direct and Indirect Methods are permitted under accounting standards, such as GAAP (ASC 230) and IFRS (IAS 7), providing companies with flexibility in presentation. However, since the Indirect Method is generally preferred due to its ease of preparation, it frequently lacks the detail required for thorough legal analysis.

In litigation, such as calculating damages for lost operating cash flow, assessing solvency in bankruptcy, or investigating fraud (e.g., the red flags outlined in subchapter 7 ahead), lawyers must understand the sources and uses of cash.

For example, in a breach-of-contract case, determining the exact cash lost from a client relationship requires knowing actual collections, not only accrual adjustments. A supplemental schedule of significant cash receipts and payments provides this detail, breaking down cash inflows (e.g., $400,000 from Customer A) and outflows (e.g., $200,000 to Supplier B). Requesting this schedule ensures lawyers have the granular data needed to build a robust case, especially when the Indirect Method's reconciliation obscures critical cash flow patterns, such as those tied to aging receivables or fraudulent revenue recognition.

This comparison underscores the trade-offs between the Direct and Indirect Methods, highlighting their implications for financial transparency and legal analysis. While the Indirect Method is more commonly used and easier to prepare, its lack of detail can impede investigations into cash flow dynamics, which is an important matter in legal contexts such as damages calculations or fraud detection.

4 The Indirect Method - Step by Step

The Indirect Method provides a systematic approach to converting accrual-based net income into cash-based operating cash flow, thereby revealing the cash generated from core operations.

For lawyers, this process is invaluable in various legal contexts, such as assessing solvency in bankruptcy (where a positive OCF indicates viability), ensuring covenant compliance (where lenders may require a minimum OCF), or calculating damages for lost cash flows in litigation (as noted in subsection 2).

4.1 Start with Net Income (bottom line of the P&L).

Net Income is the final profit figure from the income statement (as seen in the ABC Law LLP P&L in the Income Statement chapter, where net income was $99,000).

Net income is calculated under the accrual basis of accounting, which includes non-cash items and timing differences (e.g., revenue earned but not yet received).

Net income is the starting point because it represents the accrual-based performance of the company, which must be adjusted to reflect actual cash movements in the operating activities section.

A word of caution: Because the indirect method starts from the income statement's Net Income, any inaccuracies or manipulations in the income statement will "flow" to the operating activities cash flow. Therefore, the operating cash flow is not "bullet-proof," so to speak.

4.2 Add back non-cash expenses

Non-cash expenses reduce net income but do not involve actual cash outflows, so they are added back to reflect the cash available from operations.

- **Depreciation and amortization**

These expenses allocate the cost of tangible assets (e.g., depreciation of equipment) and intangible assets (e.g., amortization of patents) over their useful lives.

For example, if ABC Law LLP reports $20,000 in depreciation for office equipment, this amount reduces net income but does not involve the use of cash, so it's added back. The tip box, "Depreciation is Positive!" (Figure 4.6), reinforces this: Depreciation lowers net income without consuming cash, making it a positive adjustment in the cash-flow statement.

- **Non-cash share-based compensation**

Non-Cash Share-Based Compensation: This includes stock options or equity grants given to employees, which are recorded as an expense but do not involve cash payments. If a company reports $10,000 in share-based compensation, this amount is added back because it reduces net income without affecting cash.

4.3 Subtract non-cash gains (e.g., unrealized FX gains).

Non-cash gains increase net income but do not generate cash, so they are subtracted to avoid overstating cash flow.

For example, an unrealized foreign exchange (FX) gain occurs when the value of foreign currency holdings increases due to changes in the exchange rate, without any actual cash exchange. If a company reports a $15,000 unrealized FX gain, this amount is subtracted because it's not cash received from core operations.

4.4 Adjust for working-capital changes

Working capital changes reflect the timing differences between when transactions are recorded (under the accrual and matching principles) and when cash is actually exchanged. These adjustments ensure the cash-flow statement captures the actual cash impact of operations.

- **Increase in Accounts Receivable → subtract (cash not yet collected)**

An increase in accounts receivable means the company recorded revenue (boosting net income) but hasn't collected the cash.

For example, if receivables increase by $30,000, this amount is subtracted because the cash is still owed by customers, tying up liquidity.

- **Increase in Accounts Payable → add (cash not yet paid)**

An increase in accounts payable indicates that the company owes more to suppliers but hasn't yet paid, thereby preserving cash. If payables increase by $20,000, this amount is added back because the cash remains in the company's possession.

- **Inventory, prepaid expenses, and accrued liabilities follow the same logic.**

The same principle applies to other working capital items.

An increase in inventory (e.g., $25,000) is subtracted because cash was spent to acquire goods that have not yet been sold.

A decrease in prepaid expenses (e.g., $10,000) is added because the company no longer needs to set aside cash for those prepayments.

An increase in accrued liabilities (e.g., $15,000 in unpaid wages) is added because the expense reduced net income, but the cash hasn't been paid out.

> **MALPRACTICE ALERT: Misreading Working Capital**

In M&A or litigation, lawyers who ignore working capital shifts risk massive valuation errors. A positive net income with ballooning receivables is a warning sign, not a win. Ask: "Where's the cash?" not only "Where's the profit?"

4.5 Result: Cash Provided by Operating Activities (OCF)

After making the adjustments, adding back non-cash expenses, subtracting non-cash gains, and adjusting for working capital changes, the result is the Cash Provided by Operating Activities (OCF).

This figure represents the net cash generated (or used) by the company's main or core operations. A positive cash flow from operations (OCF) indicates that the company can fund its operations with cash generated from its primary activities, a key sign of financial health.

A negative OCF, especially alongside positive net income, is a red flag (as noted before), potentially indicating issues like uncollectible receivables or overstocked inventory, which could signal fraud or insolvency.

4.6 Add the Investing and Financing sections to calculate the Net Change in Cash.

The OCF is combined with the cash flows from investing activities (e.g., buying or selling assets) and financing activities (e.g., borrowing or paying dividends) to calculate the net change in cash for the period.

This net change is added to the opening cash balance to determine the closing cash balance, thereby reconciling the cash-flow statement with the balance sheet.

For example, if the OCF is $100,000, the investing cash flow is -$50,000 (due to equipment purchases), and the financing cash flow is $30,000 (from a new loan), the net change in cash is $80,000, which adjusts the opening cash to the closing cash balance.

Depreciation is Positive!

Because depreciation reduces net income without using cash, you add it back.

Figure 4.6: TIP. Depreciation

As mentioned before, this tip reinforces a key concept: Depreciation (and similar non-cash expenses, such as amortization) reduces net income on the income statement but does not involve a cash outflow.

Lawyer's Tip

Solvency analysis shortcuts: Essential calculations for immediate assessment:

- Operating Cash Margin = OCF ÷ Revenue (below 5% = warning)
- Free Cash Flow = OCF - CapEx (negative = unsustainable)
- Cash Interest Coverage = OCF ÷ Interest Paid (below 2x = danger)
- Board minutes discussing cash management decisions

Document demand: Request 24+ months of monthly cash flow detail

---

Lawyer Application

Operating Cash Flow in Valuation & Fraud

- **Due diligence: Steady OCF confirms a reliable earnings base.**

- **Red flags: A sharp drop in OCF, despite stable revenue, suggests inflated earnings or channel stuffing.**

- **Contractual triggers: Tie earn-outs to cash metrics, not net income, to avoid manipulation.**

5 Key Cash Metrics for Lawyers

Metric	Formula	Why It Matters
Operating-Cash Margin	OCF ÷ Revenue	Tests earnings quality in valuation and damage awards.
Free Cash Flow (FCF)	OCF – Capital Expenditures	Dividend capacity, equity valuation, M&A price adjustments.
Cash-Interest Coverage	OCF ÷ Interest Paid in Cash	Preferred lender covenant; ignores non-cash earnings.
Levered FCF	FCF – Mandatory Debt Service	Core test in solvency opinions and fraudulent-transfer litigation.

Figure 4.7: Key Cash Metrics for Lawyers

Figure 4.7 outlines four essential cash flow metrics: Operating Cash Margin, Free Cash Flow (FCF), Cash Interest Coverage, and Levered FCF, that lawyers can use to assess a company's financial health and liquidity.

Building on the cash-flow statement concepts introduced in subchapters 1 through 4, these metrics distill cash flow data into practical ratios, providing insights into earnings quality, dividend capacity, debt servicing ability, and solvency.

For lawyers, these metrics are crucial tools in various legal contexts, including valuation disputes, damages calculations, covenant compliance, solvency opinions, and fraudulent transfer litigation.

By focusing on cash-based metrics rather than accrual-based profits, which offer a more accurate representation of a company's financial reality, lawyers can identify issues that may lead to disputes or regulatory reviews.

- **Operating-Cash Margin = OCF ÷ Revenue**

This metric measures the percentage of revenue that translates into cash flow from operating activities (OCF), which is calculated using the Indirect Method (as detailed in subchapter 4).

For example, if a company has an OCF of $200,000 and revenue of $1,000,000, its Operating-Cash Margin is 20%, meaning $0.20 of every revenue dollar becomes operating cash.

Why it matters: The Operating-Cash Margin test assesses earnings quality in valuation and damage awards.

A high margin indicates that reported revenue (accrual-based) is converting efficiently into cash, supporting the reliability of earnings in valuation disputes (e.g., determining a fair price in M&A litigation).

In damage awards, such as breach-of-contract cases, it helps quantify the cash impact of lost revenue, ensuring awards reflect actual liquidity losses rather than inflated accrual profits.

A low or negative margin, especially alongside high net income, aligns with the red flags in subchapter 7 (e.g., revenue growth outpacing operating cash), potentially signaling issues like uncollectible receivables or fraudulent revenue recognition.

- **Free Cash Flow (FCF) = OCF − Capital Expenditures**

Free Cash Flow (FCF) is the cash remaining after subtracting capital expenditures (capex, such as buying equipment or property, reported in the investing activities section) from OCF.

For instance, if the OCF is $200,000 and the capital expenditure is $50,000, the free cash flow (FCF) is $150,000.

Why it matters: FCF measures the cash available for discretionary uses, making it crucial for dividend capacity (how much a company can pay in dividends without straining operations), equity valuation (as a basis for discounted cash flow models in M&A or shareholder disputes), and M&A price adjustments (e.g., adjusting the purchase price based on available cash).

Lawyers use FCF in shareholder lawsuits to assess whether dividends were paid responsibly or if needed capital expenditures were deferred, potentially breaching fiduciary obligations.

A negative FCF might indicate overinvestment or operational inefficiencies, prompting further investigation in legal contexts.

- **Cash-Interest Coverage = OCF ÷ Interest Paid in Cash**

This metric divides OCF by the interest paid in cash (from the financing activities section or supplemental disclosures), focusing solely on cash-based interest payments rather than accrual-based interest expense.

For example, if the OCF is $200,000 and the cash interest paid is $40,000, the Cash-Interest Coverage ratio is 5×, meaning the company generates five times the cash needed to cover interest payments.

Why it matters: This is a preferred lender covenant because it ignores non-cash earnings (e.g., depreciation or unrealized gains), providing a stricter test of a company's ability to service debt with actual cash, as opposed to the EBIT-based interest-coverage ratio.

In legal contexts, a low ratio may signal a breach of covenant, leading to disputes with lenders.

It's also critical in solvency assessments, as it shows whether a company can meet interest obligations without relying on financing or asset sales, a key concern in bankruptcy proceedings.

- **Levered FCF = FCF − Mandatory Debt Service**

Levered Free Cash Flow (Levered FCF) subtracts mandatory debt service (principal repayments and interest, typically found in the financing activities section) from FCF.

For example, if FCF is $150,000 and mandatory debt service is $60,000, Levered FCF is $90,000.

Why it matters: This metric is a core test in solvency opinions and fraudulent-transfer litigation.

A positive Levered FCF indicates the company can meet its debt obligations and still have cash for operations, supporting its solvency in bankruptcy cases. In fraudulent-transfer litigation, it's used to assess whether payments, such as dividends, were made while the company was insolvent.

For instance, if a company with a negative Levered Free Cash Flow (FCF) pays a $100,000 dividend, creditors might argue that this constitutes a fraudulent transfer and seek recovery of these funds.

This metric enables lawyers to assess whether a company's cash flows support its financial decisions, thereby protecting stakeholders from improper transactions.

In Short

These cash metrics provide a cash-based perspective on a company's financial health, complementing the accrual-based income statement and balance sheet.

For lawyers, they are indispensable in legal contexts where cash flow drives outcomes, whether valuing a business, calculating damages, ensuring covenant compliance, or assessing solvency. They also relate to the red flags discussed in subchapter 7, such as discrepancies between net income and operating cash flow.

By focusing on actual cash movements, these metrics enable lawyers to uncover financial realities that accrual accounting may obscure.

6 Case Illustration - ABC Law PLL, Second Quarter

Returning to ABC Law LLP, we see that after a strong Q1 on paper, their cash-flow statement tells a different story—one that could influence their next loan approval or partner confidence. Here is how their performance appears in cash.

CASH FLOW STATEMENT

Cash Source (Use)	Amount ($'000)
NET INCOME (accrual)	99
+ Depreciation (IT gear)	18
– Increase in Accounts Receivable	(110)
– Increase in Work-in-Progress	(45)
+ Increase in Accounts Payable	35
OPERATING CASH FLOW	(3)
– Purchase of Legal-Tech Software	(21)
FREE CASH FLOW	(24)
+ Partner Capital Contribution	50
– Partner Draws & Tax Distributions	(60)
NET CHANGE IN CASH	(34)

Figure 4.8: Cash Flow Statement

Figure 4.8 presents a cash-flow statement for ABC Law LLP for the second quarter, using the Indirect Method to calculate cash flow from operating activities, followed by investing and financing activities to determine the net change in cash. All amounts are in thousands of U.S. dollars (USD '000).

This illustration builds on the ABC Law LLP P&L statement, where net income was $99,000, and applies the cash-flow concepts introduced in subchapters 1 through 5, including the three cash buckets, the Indirect Method, and key cash metrics.

The interpretation highlights the firm's liquidity challenges despite profitability, a recurring theme in this book, and emphasizes the legal and financial risks linked to cash flow mismanagement, such as covenant breaches or partner disputes.

- **Net Income (Accrual)**

The starting point is ABC Law's net profit of **$ 99,000** from the P&L. Because it is accrual-based, it records revenue earned and expenses incurred regardless of when cash moves. This on-paper profit must be reconciled to actual cash.

- **Depreciation (IT Gear)**

Depreciation of $18,000 for IT equipment (e.g., computers and servers) is a non-cash expense that reduces net income but does not involve a cash outflow. As explained in subchapter 4, depreciation is added back to net income because it represents a cost allocation rather than a cash expenditure, ensuring that the cash-flow statement accurately reflects the cash available from operations. This adjustment increases the cash flow calculation by $18,000.

- **Increase in Accounts Receivable**

An increase in accounts receivable of $110,000 indicates that ABC Law recorded $110,000 more in revenue than it collected in cash during the quarter. This reflects sluggish collections, as clients owe the firm more at the end of the quarter than at the beginning, thereby tying up liquidity.

Following the Indirect Method in subchapter 4, this increase is subtracted because the cash has not yet been received, reducing the operating cash flow by $110,000. This significant increase in receivables aligns with the red flags in subchapter 7, such as receivables aging, which can signal potential issues with revenue quality or collectability.

- **Increase in Work-in-Progress**

An increase in work-in-progress (WIP) of $45,000 represents unbilled legal work that has accumulated during the quarter. In a law firm like ABC Law, WIP includes hours worked on client matters that have not yet been invoiced.

In the indirect method, this increase is subtracted from net income in the cash flow statement as no cash has been received yet. Note that the expenses that the firm incurred (e.g., associate wages) to perform the WIP are reflected in net income, in application of the accrual and matching principles. If a portion of these wages remains unpaid, that liability will appear in accounts payable and be added back in the cash flow statement.

As noted earlier, overstating WIP can inflate gross profit in the income statement (accrual accounting). However, when it comes to the cash flow statement, the trick does not work: Any increase in WIP is subtracted in the operating section, ensuring that only cash received is reflected in operating cash flow.

- **Increase in Accounts Payable**

An increase in accounts payable of $35,000 means ABC Law owes more to suppliers or vendors (e.g., for outsourcing or office expenses) at the end of the quarter than at the beginning.

This increase is added back to the cash flow calculation because the firm has not yet paid these expenses, preserving cash in the short term. As explained in subchapter 4, this adjustment reflects the timing difference between expense recognition (under the matching principle) and actual cash payment, increasing operating cash flow by $35,000.

- **Operating Cash Flow**

-$3,000 of cash emerged from core operations, despite a $99,000 profit, evidence that earnings quality is weak, highlighting liquidity challenges due to slow collections and rising WIP, a concern that echoes the red flags in subchapter 7 (e.g., positive net income with low operating cash flow).

- **Purchase of Legal-Tech Software**

This $21,000 cash outflow, recorded in the investing activities section, reflects the purchase of legal-tech software, a capital expenditure (capex) to enhance the firm's operations (e.g., case management tools). This investment reduces cash but is not part of operating activities, as it pertains to long-term assets rather than day-to-day operations.

- **Free Cash Flow**

No discretionary cash is available, leaving no buffer for unexpected expenses or investments.

- **Partner Capital Contribution**

This $50,000 cash inflow, recorded in the Financing Activities section, represents new capital contributed by partners to the firm, which may be used to support operations or fund the purchase of software. It increases available cash but also reflects reliance on partner funding rather than operational cash flow, a sign of underlying liquidity constraints.

- **Partner Draws & Tax Distributions**

This $60,000 cash outflow, also in the Financing Activities section, includes partner draws (distributions of profit to partners) and tax distributions (payments to cover partners' tax liabilities). As noted, partner draws are treated as equity distributions, not expenses, and occur after net income. Equity distributions consume more cash than the business produces.

It is worth noting that since partners retired $50,000 from the business, their net contribution to the business is $10,000.

- **Net Change in Cash**

Cash fell **$34,000** for the quarter.

Interpretation: Profitable on Paper, but Sluggish Collections and Rising WIP Choke Liquidity with no Residual Cash.

ABC Law reports **$99k** in accrued profit, but collections lag (**+$110k AR**) and rising WIP (**+$45k**) drain liquidity; operating activities burn **$3k**.

After funding minimal capital expenditures and paying partner draws, the cash balance drops by **$34,000**.

If collections don't improve, the firm may struggle to meet its obligations, potentially breaching loan covenants (such as the interest-coverage covenant in the exercises) or prompting partner disputes over distributions.

Legally, this situation could lead to scrutiny in solvency opinions (if the firm faces creditor claims) or fraudulent-transfer litigation (if draws are deemed excessive while the firm is insolvent).

This illustration highlights the disconnect between accrual-based profitability and cash-based liquidity, a recurring theme in the book.

For lawyers, capturing these relationships is important in situations such as covenant compliance, where low cash flow may lead to a default, or in litigation, where slow collections could influence damage calculations.

By analyzing ABC Law's cash-flow statement, you can see how operational inefficiencies and financing decisions impact liquidity, reinforcing the importance of cash flow analysis in both financial and legal accountability.

CASH FLOW STATEMENT

ITEM	AMOUNT (US$ '000)
Net Income	99
Depreciation	+18
Increase in AR	(110)
Increase in WIP	(45)
Increase in AP	+35
Operating Cash Flow	(3)

Figure 4.9: Statement of Cash Flows

7 Cash-flow Statement Red-Flag Checklist for Lawyers

The following checklist highlights critical cash flow warning signs that lawyers should monitor when reviewing financial statements.

These indicators can reveal hidden liquidity problems, operational instability, or financial manipulation: Issues that may trigger covenant breaches, litigation, or insolvency proceedings. Each red flag corresponds to one of the three cash flow categories (subchapter 2) or key performance metrics (subchapter 5), surfacing risks that accrual-based statements can obscure, such as unsustainable dividends or off-balance sheet financing.

For legal professionals involved in litigation, due diligence, or restructuring, identifying these signs early is crucial. In bankruptcy, persistent negative cash flow may confirm insolvency; in fraudulent-transfer cases, dividend-funded asset sales may be reversed; in valuation disputes, weak cash generation often undermines headline profits. Ignoring these patterns can expose clients to regulatory scrutiny, mounting liability, or reputational damage.

By integrating cash flow analysis into your legal toolkit, you not only protect stakeholders and ensure contractual compliance, but you also **enhance your value as a legal advisor**, sharpen your ability to detect financial misrepresentation, and position yourself as a more **strategic, competitive, and trusted professional** in any high-stakes matter. That is the core objective of this book.

Red-Flag Checklist for Lawyers

🚩 Operating cash negative two years running while net income positive

🚩 Revenue up 20 %, AR Days Outstanding up from 45 to 75

🚩 Proceeds from asset sales fund dividends ("selling the furniture to pay rent")

🚩 Financing inflows every quarter just to cover operating losses

🚩 Capitalised interest masks the true interest burden

Figure 4.10: Red-Flag Checklist for Lawyers. Cash Flows

Operating Cash Negative Two Years Running While Net Income Positive: This red flag occurs when a company reports positive net income (indicating profitability on an accrual basis) but negative cash flow from operating activities (OCF) for two consecutive years.

As discussed, OCF is calculated by adjusting net income for non-cash items and working capital changes, revealing the cash generated from core operations. A sustained mismatch between positive net income and negative OCF, echoing the ABC Law LLP case (subchapter 6), where OCF was -$3,000 despite a net income of $99,000, suggests issues such as uncollectible receivables, inventory buildup, or aggressive revenue recognition.

Another example is a software company that books $2 million in license revenue but only collects $500,000 in cash, creating a $1.5

million receivables problem that compounds over time.

This pattern frequently precedes bankruptcy filings and creates legal exposure in multiple areas: Securities litigation, where shareholders claim earnings manipulation; preference payment recovery in bankruptcy, where recent payments become vulnerable; and director liability cases, where continued operations while cash flow insolvent may breach fiduciary duties.

Courts can view sustained negative operating cash flow as evidence of insolvency, making this metric critical in fraudulent transfer litigation, where the timing of insolvency determines legal exposure.

Revenue Up 20%, AR Days Outstanding Up from 45 to 75: This warning sign indicates a significant increase in revenue (20%) accompanied by a corresponding rise in Accounts Receivable (AR) Days Outstanding, from 45 to 75 days. AR Days Outstanding measures how long it takes to collect cash from customers (calculated as (Accounts Receivable ÷ Revenue) × 365), and an increase from 45 to 75 days indicates slower collections; customers are taking longer to pay.

Despite the revenue growth, the cash isn't coming in, as evidenced by ABC Law's $110,000 increase in receivables (subchapter 6) (e.g., receivables aging), which potentially indicates relaxed credit terms, uncollectible accounts, or fictitious sales, all of which can artificially inflate revenue.

Legally, this creates multiple risks: Disputes over revenue quality in M&A transactions where earn-outs depend on sales metrics, damages calculations in breach of contract cases where uncollectible receivables overstate losses, and securities fraud investigations where revenue recognition practices may violate accounting standards.

The disconnect between revenue growth and cash collection often triggers auditor scrutiny and can lead to restatements, exposing companies to shareholder lawsuits.

Proceeds from Asset Sales Funding Dividends ("Selling the Furniture to Pay Rent"): This red flag occurs when a company uses proceeds from asset sales (reported in the Investing Activities section, as per subchapter 2) to fund dividend payments (in the Financing Activities section).

The metaphor "selling the furniture to pay rent" illustrates the unsustainable practice of liquidating long-term assets to cover short-term obligations, such as dividends. For example, if a company sells $100,000 in equipment to pay a $90,000 dividend, it may be masking operational weaknesses.

Legally, this can lead to shareholder lawsuits alleging mismanagement, especially if the company's core operations (OCF) are unprofitable, or fraudulent-transfer claims in bankruptcy, where creditors might argue that dividends paid with asset sale proceeds were improper if the company was insolvent at the time.

Financing Inflows Every Quarter Just to Cover Operating Losses: This warning sign indicates a company is consistently relying on financing activities (e.g., borrowing or issuing equity) to offset negative operating cash flow.

For instance, if a company has an OCF of -$50,000 each quarter and borrows $60,000 to cover it, this pattern suggests the core business is not self-sustaining, a concern echoed in ABC Law's negative OCF and partner contribution (subchapter 6). This reliance on external funding, as highlighted in the Financing Activities section, raises concerns about the long-term viability of the business.

For lawyers, this can signal insolvency in bankruptcy proceedings, as the company cannot fund operations internally, or a breach of covenants requiring a minimum OCF. It may also prompt due diligence concerns in M&A, where buyers assess whether the target's growth is debt-funded and unsustainable.

Capitalized Interest Masking True Interest Burden: This red flag involves capitalizing interest (treating it as part of an asset's cost, such as for a construction project, rather than an expense), which reduces reported interest expense in the income statement and financing cash outflows.

As noted earlier, this practice can inflate operating income and understate the true cost of debt. For example, if a company capitalizes $30,000 of interest that should have been expensed, its Cash-Interest Coverage ratio (OCF ÷ Interest Paid in Cash, as per subchapter 5) appears stronger than it actually is, masking the real interest burden.

Legally, this can lead to covenant breaches if lenders rely on accurate interest coverage ratios (as in the ABC Law covenant check exercise) or misrepresentation claims in shareholder litigation if the company's debt burden is understated. It's also a concern in solvency opinions, as capitalized interest can obscure the company's ability to service debt with operational cash.

8 Stories from the Trenches

Inventory Mirage: An appliance wholesaler employed FIFO accounting during inflation to boost profits by $4 million over a two-year period; however, operating cash flow turned negative as inventory consumed all available cash. When the lender added a 2.5x interest-coverage covenant, the company missed it by $400,000 in the first quarter. Result: Immediate default, asset-based lending conversion, and $1 million in legal fees fighting foreclosure proceedings

Dividend-Paid-with-Debt LBO: Private equity extracted $120 million via a new term loan. Levered free cash flow turned negative; two years later, the company defaulted. Creditors sued under fraudulent transfer theories, and cash-flow projections presented at closing became Exhibit A.

Trust-Account Violation: A small firm showed positive operating cash only because it raided client retainers. The cash-flow statement lacked a separate IOLTA (an account required in many jurisdictions where lawyers must hold client funds separately). Misusing IOLTA funds is considered a form of misappropriation. In this case, the state bar imposed a suspension and restitution.

9 How the Three Statements Talk to One Another

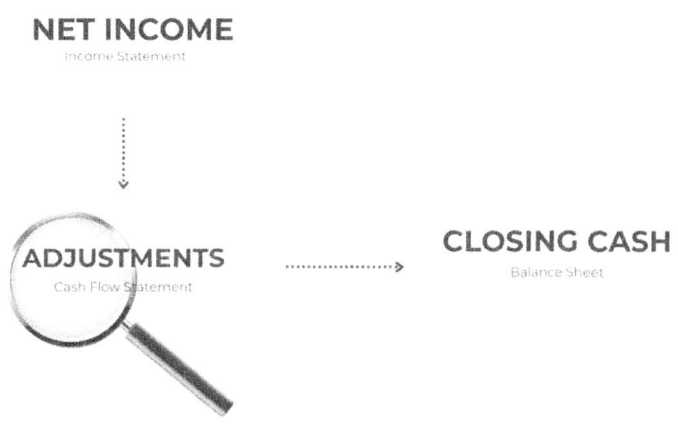

Figure 4.11: Net Income, Adjustments, Closing Cash

9.1 Income - Cash Flow:
Net income is the starting point of the OCF; widening gaps demand explanation.

9.2 Cash Flow -Balance Sheet:
The net change in cash appears as the difference between the opening and closing cash lines; the Investing and Financing sections reveal why debt or equity changed.

9.3 Triangulation Rule:
If two statements agree and the third does not, dig into the odd one -

it's typically where errors or fraud hide.

Key Takeaways

- Profit can be engineered far longer than cash.
- OCF is the lawyer's first solvency test and the lender's favorite covenant.
- Working-capital changes tell a truth that income statements hide - trace them invoice by invoice.
- FCF, not EBITDA, funds dividends, debt service, and settlement cheques.

Callback

The biotech firm eventually raised bridge capital - but only after incurring severe dilution and reputational damage. All because no one paid attention to the cash-flow statement.

In finance, profit is hope. Cash is power.

The **income statement** tells us whether a company appears profitable. The **cash-flow statement** shows whether that profit is real or an illusion.

Final Thoughts

When ABC Law LLP first opened its doors, its partners were experienced attorneys, but they did not know how to read the numbers.

Now, after critical missteps, they understand **that cash can disappear even when income appears strong** and that **debt on a balance sheet is more than just a number; it's a covenant**.

They also understand that a clean income statement and balance sheets can still hide trouble in the footnotes, timing games, or the flow of funds.

These three financial statements, when read together, not only describe a business. They **tell its story, whisper its risks, and forecast its future**.

And now, as a lawyer, you, in contrast to the partners of ABC Law LLP, possess the skills to read that story fluently, help your clients, and manage your business in a way that much of your competition can't.

You can spot red flags, ask smarter questions, negotiate from insight, and protect your clients and yourself from dangerous illusions masked by accounting tricks.

You didn't need to become an accountant. You just needed to become fluent in the language of business to become a **trusted advisor** in deals, litigation, or restructurings.

Follow the money, and you'll never be misled.

10 Exercises

10.1 OCF Red Flag

A company reports $500,000 net income but -$200,000 OCF. What questions should a lawyer ask in due diligence?

10.2 Fraudulent Transfer Test
A firm borrows $1M to pay a dividend while technically insolvent. How could creditors use the cash-flow statement in court?

10.3 Direct vs. Indirect
You're given only the Indirect Method. What schedule would you demand to verify cash receipts in litigation?

6 CONCLUSIONS: FROM LINGERING DOUBT TO FINANCIAL INSIGHT – YOUR NEW INDISPENSABLE SKILL

Remember that 11:42 p.m. email: The one that landed like a ticking clock, threatening to derail the deal with a "minor update" to the balance sheet? Tripled liabilities. No explanation. No footnote. In that moment, financial literacy was the difference between panic and clarity.

By 11:47 p.m., a focused review revealed what happened: A supplier had accelerated payment terms, converting long-term debt into a material current liability. The signing was rescheduled, the price dropped by $2 million to account for the hidden liability, and the client avoided a potential bankruptcy trap, all because one lawyer understood what the numbers meant.

That is the power this book has aimed to put in your hands.

Core Lessons to Carry Forward

- **The Principles Govern Everything:**

Revenue recognition, matching, and conservatism aren't abstract concepts; they're the rules that determine whether those statements tell the truth or hide it. Violations of these principles are where litigation begins.

- **The balance sheet is Your Snapshot:**

One page shows what a company owns, what it owes, and what's left for its owners. Assets = Liabilities + Equity is not a theory; it's your solvency test, red-flag detector, and negotiation tool.

- **The income statement is the Story:**

Revenues, expenses, and net income reveal performance over time. But remember: Accrual accounting allows manipulation. From "phantom invoices" to aggressive revenue recognition, this is where footprints of fraud often appear.

- **The cash-flow statement Reveals Reality:**

Profit is opinion; cash is fact. By breaking movements into operating, investing, and financing activities, this statement shows whether profit translates into liquidity. Watch for the classic danger sign: Positive net income with negative operating cash flow.

- **The three statements Interconnect:**

They tell a unified story. If two line up but the third doesn't, dig deeper; that's generally where the truth hides.

Putting It into Practice

The next time a financial statement crosses your desk in due diligence, discovery, or even your own firm's reports, don't file it away. Open it. Engage with it. Ask:

- **What does this entity own, and what does it owe?**
- **How did it perform, and did performance translate into cash?**
- **Do the red-flag checklists reveal anything unusual?**
- **Which ratios confirm or challenge the story being told?**

Start tomorrow. Pull the last financial statement you encountered, whether from a deal, a case file, or your own firm. Apply just one tool from this book: Calculate the current ratio, check operating cash flow versus net income, or scan for 'Other' items over 10%. That single action transforms theory into practice.

You've invested hours in mastering these concepts; that investment pays dividends with every financial statement you'll ever encounter.

You now have the tools to question assumptions, trace the money, and connect financial dots to legal realities. The "five minutes with the numbers" that can save a client, a deal, or your reputation are within your grasp.

Your Financial Literacy Journey Continues

This book gave you the foundation. To maintain your edge:

- **Review one financial statement monthly.**
- **Build your own template library from the tools provided.**
- **Share insights with colleagues: Teaching solidifies learning.**
- **Track how many times financial literacy changes your legal strategy.**

Join our community at www.ramonandrade.com for updates on accounting changes that affect legal practice, downloadable templates, and exclusive case studies.

The 30-Day Challenge

For the next 30 days, apply one concept from this book to every financial document you encounter. Track your insights. At month's end, you'll be amazed at how naturally financial analysis has become part of your legal thinking.

Final Word

The world of accounting will continue to evolve, but the fundamentals remain: What a business owns, owes, earns, and burns. Mastering these basics elevates you from lawyer to trusted advisor, one who sees what others miss.

What once looked like foreign numbers is now a language you command. And when you can read the story behind the numbers, you not only practice law, but practice it with power.

The next time you're in a conference room at 11:42 p.m. and the numbers don't add up, you won't feel that stomach-dropping dread. You'll feel something else entirely: Confidence, because you'll know exactly which questions to ask, which documents to demand, and which red flags to hunt.

That transformation, from financial anxiety to financial authority, is your competitive advantage in modern legal practice.

7 APPENDICES

Appendix A – References & Recommended Reading

This appendix provides a curated list of references, resources, and further readings that support the concepts discussed in *The Busy Attorney's Guide to Financial Statements*. These materials are not exhaustive, but they represent authoritative sources for deepening your understanding of accounting and financial statement analysis in a legal context.

Primary Accounting Standards & Frameworks
- International Accounting Standards Board (IASB). *International Financial Reporting Standards (IFRS)*. https://www.ifrs.org.
- Financial Accounting Standards Board (FASB). *Generally Accepted Accounting Principles (GAAP)*. https://www.fasb.org.

Legal & Professional References
- American Bar Association (ABA). Lawyer's Guide to Business & Accounting.

- Black, H.C. Black's Law Dictionary. 11th Edition.

Public Companies, Firms & Cases Mentioned

- Boeing Company – SEC Filings and Annual Reports. https://investors.boeing.com.
- Clifford Chance LLP – Global law firm resources and publications. https://www.cliffordchance.com; https://www.cliffordchance.com/content/dam/cliffordchance/About_us/responsible-business/2021/statutory-financial-accounts-2021.pdf.
- Coca-Cola – https://www.nasdaq.com/market-activity/stocks/ko/financials.
- Enron Corporation (historical case) – SEC archives and case studies on corporate fraud. https://www.sec.gov/spotlight/enron.htm.
- Lehman Brothers (2008 bankruptcy case) – Court filings and examiner's report. https://www.jenner.com/en/news-insights/news/lehman-brothers-holdings-inc-chapter-11-proceedings-examiner-s-report.
- Linklaters LLP – Thought leadership and financial/legal publications. https://www.linklaters.com; https://find-and-update.company-information.service.gov.uk/company/OC326345/filing-history.
- WorldCom (historical case) – DOJ and SEC filings; classic example of accounting fraud. https://www.sec.gov/enforcement-litigation/litigation-releases/lr-17588.

Articles & Commentary

Boeing

- Infortal Global. *A Matter of Survival for Boeing.* https://infortal.com/a-matter-of-survival-for-boeing/.
- Kavout. *How Boeing's Safety Issues and DOJ Settlement Talks are Influencing Stock Performance.* https://www.kavout.com/market-lens/how-boeings-safety-issues-and-doj-settlement-talks-are-influencing-stock-performance.

Enron
- FBI. *Enron Case Overview.* https://www.fbi.gov/history/famous-cases/enron
- SEC. *Press Release 2004-18 (Enforcement Action).* https://www.sec.gov/news/press/2004-18.htm.

Lehman Brothers
- SEC. *Complaint No. 18116 (Corporate Fraud Case).* https://www.sec.gov/litigation/complaints/comp18116.htm.

Tyco
- SEC. *Litigation Release No. 19657.* https://www.sec.gov/enforcement-litigation/litigation-releases/lr-19657.
- SEC. *Tyco International Enforcement Action.* https://www.sec.gov/divisions/enforce/claims/tyco.htm.

WorldCom
- SEC. Complaint No. 17829 (Corporate Fraud Case). https://www.sec.gov/litigation/complaints/comp17829.htm.

Textbooks & Guides
- Altman, Edward I., and Hotchkiss, Edith. *Corporate Financial Distress and Bankruptcy.* 3rd Edition. Wiley, 2006
- Anthony, Robert N., et al. *Accounting: Text and Cases.* 11th Edition. McGraw-Hill, 2003.
- Bodie, Kane, and Marcus. *Essentials of Investments.* 5th Edition. McGraw-Hill, 2003.
- Damodaran, Aswath. *Applied Corporate Finance: A User's Manual.* 2nd Edition. Wiley, 2006
- Damodaran, Aswath. *Investment Valuation: Tools and Techniques for Determining the Value of Any Asset.* 2nd Edition. Wiley, 2002.
- Fraser, Lyn M., and Ormiston, Aileen. *Understanding Financial Statements.* 12th Edition. Pearson, 2024.
- Mathew Barrett J. et al. *Accounting for Lawyers, Conise.* 6th Edition. Foundation Press, 2022.

- Stickney, Clyde, et al. *Financial Accounting: An Introduction to Concepts, Methods, and Uses.* 14th Edition. Cengage, 2009.
- Wisniewski, Mik. *Quantitative Methods for Decision Makers.* 4th Edition. Prentice Hall, Financial Times, 2006.

Fraud & Forensic Accounting
- Albrecht, W. Steve, et al. Fraud Examination. 6th Edition. Cengage.
- Association of Certified Fraud Examiners (ACFE). https://www.acfe.com.
- Wells, Joseph T. Principles of Fraud Examination. 4th Edition. Wiley.

Regulatory and Professional Organizations & Resources
- American Institute of Certified Public Accountants (AICPA). https://www.aicpa.org.
- Chartered Financial Analyst (CFA) Institute. https://www.cfainstitute.org.
- Securities and Exchange Commission (SEC) – Filings & Reports. https://www.sec.gov/edgar.

Suggested Continuing Education for Attorneys
- Attorney Acceleration Institute's On-Demand Webinars: *Accounting Basics for Attorneys.*
- www.ramonandrade.com

Note for Readers: References are provided for informational purposes only. This book is designed as a practical guide and does not substitute for consulting accounting standards, auditors, or subject-matter experts in complex cases.

Appendix B – Glossary of Key Financial Terms

This glossary provides concise definitions of financial and accounting terms most relevant to legal practice.

Accrual Accounting

An accounting method where revenues and expenses are recorded when earned or incurred, regardless of when cash changes hands.

Accounts Payable (AP)

Money a company owes to suppliers or vendors for goods or services received but not yet paid for.

Accounts Receivable (AR)

Money owed to a company by its customers for goods or services already delivered.

Amortization

The gradual write-off of intangible assets (like patents) or repayment of debt over time.

Assets

Resources owned or controlled by a company that have economic value and can generate future benefits.

Balance Sheet

A financial statement showing a company's assets, liabilities, and equity at a specific point in time.

Capital Expenditures (CapEx)

Funds spent on acquiring or improving long-term assets, such as buildings or equipment.

Cash-flow statement

A report that tracks cash inflows and outflows from operations, investing, and financing activities.

Current Assets

Assets expected to be converted into cash, sold, or used up within one year.

Current Liabilities

Obligations due within one year (e.g., accounts payable, short-term loans).

Depreciation

The allocation of the cost of a tangible asset over its useful life.

EBIT (Earnings Before Interest and Taxes)

A measure of profitability often used in mergers, acquisitions, and valuation.

EBITDA (Earnings Before Interest, Taxes, Depreciation, and Amortization)

A measure of profitability often used in mergers, acquisitions, and valuation.

Equity

The residual value of assets after liabilities are subtracted; ownership interest in a company.

Expenses

Costs incurred in the process of generating revenue.

GAAP (Generally Accepted Accounting Principles)

The U.S. standards, rules, and conventions used in financial reporting.

Goodwill

An intangible asset representing the premium paid when acquiring another company above the fair value of its net assets.

IFRS (International Financial Reporting Standards)

Global accounting standards used in many countries outside the U.S.

Income Statement

A financial report summarizing revenues, expenses, and net income over a period of time.

Leverage

The use of borrowed funds (debt) to finance assets, operations, or acquisitions.

Liabilities

Obligations a company owes to creditors, suppliers, or other parties.

Liquidity

A measure of how quickly assets can be converted to cash to meet short-term obligations.

Market Capitalization (Market Cap)

The total value of a company's shares of stock, calculated as share price × number of shares.

Materiality

The significance of a financial item or error; something is "material" if it could influence decisions.

Net Income

The profit remaining after all expenses, taxes, and costs are deducted from revenues.

Operating Cash Flow

Cash generated from a company's core business activities.

Ratio Analysis

Using financial ratios (e.g., current ratio, debt-to-equity, return on equity) to evaluate performance and financial health.

Retained Earnings

Profits that a company has reinvested in the business rather than distributed as dividends.

Revenue

Income earned from the sale of goods or services.

Solvency

A company's ability to meet long-term obligations and continue operating in the future.

Working Capital

Current assets minus current liabilities; a measure of short-term liquidity.

Tip for Readers: This glossary is not exhaustive but focuses on the terms most commonly encountered by attorneys when reviewing financial statements in transactions, litigation, or compliance work.

ABOUT THE AUTHOR

In his nearly 30 years at the crossroads of law and finance, Ramón Andrade has seen a costly pattern emerge: brilliant attorneys missing critical red flags that five minutes with the numbers could have caught. He's seen tripled liabilities hidden in balance sheets, positive net income masking negative cash flow, and revenue recognition games that inflate earnings—oversights that repeatedly derail deals and cost clients millions. This book is the distillation of three decades of experience, designed to put an end to those blind spots.

A former partner at **Norton Rose Fulbright** and Head of Restructurings at **CAF – Development Bank of Latin America**,

Ramón led transactions exceeding **$400 million** across three continents. He advised Fortune 500 companies in the technology, energy, and finance sectors, earning recognition from **Chambers and Legal 500**. He holds the TRIUM Global Executive MBA from **NYU Stern, LSE, and HEC Paris**.

Today, Ramón runs his own practice and serves as Venture Partner at R3i Frontier Fund. He founded the **Attorney Acceleration Institute** to provide lawyers with the finance, leadership, and business skills that law schools don't teach—skills that have become essential for modern legal practice. From his base in Madrid, he continues advising on cross-border deals while teaching attorneys worldwide that understanding financial statements is not optional; it is about survival.

When not decoding balance sheets or negotiating deals, you'll find him exploring Madrid's hidden tapas bars or planning the next adventure with his wife and family.

The conversation continues at **www.ramonandrade.com**. To download your complimentary "Quick Kit" with templates and checklists mentioned in this book, and to receive updates on new case studies, please visit www.landing.ramonandrade.com/quick-kit.

Made in the USA
Coppell, TX
31 January 2026

70651413R00105